HUMAN NATURE

IS IT POSSIBLE TO CHANGE IT?

HUMAN NATURE

IS IT POSSIBLE TO CHANGE IT?

Jennifer K Smith Chong & Dennis K Chong

in unum omnes

Published by C-Jade Publications Inc.
Oakville, Ontario

Printed in Ontario, Canada

Cover by Meghan Behse, based on an original design by Hashan Shen

ISBN 978-0-9695594-7-4 (paperback)

We dedicate this work to Marcel Danesi, FRSC, PhD

Table of Contents

Preface

In our work *Do You Know How Another Knows to Be?*, we mapped the structural elements by which a person gets the knowledge, **unconsciously**, *to-know-how-to-be* in any context — whether having tea with the King of England or drinking with chums at the Grey Goose pub. These structural elements comprise our two embedded blueprints: (1) the Holarchy of Paradigms (HOPs), which we use to understand ourselves, others, and the world we live in, and (2) our embedded Ancillary 14 (An^{Y}14), which we use to define our individuality. Originally, there were only 9 (An^{Y}9). However, just as life is ever-changing, there is no discovery in the field of Epiepistemology — also known as Neuro-Semantic Programming™ (NSP) — that is written in stone. There are always new discoveries.

Our HOPs and the An^{Y}14 form our Orthodoxy, which enables us to take action. Our Orthodoxy is a function of our Being-to-the-contexts in our life. Put simply, our Orthodoxy produces our Human Nature (HN) to a given life situation of goals, wants, desires, and so forth. Nested in our Orthodoxy is a second component — **to-know**-*to-know-to-be;* rather than to-know-to-be (the way we are, our Being). The extension is about our action. It is thanks to this second component that we know to express our Human Nature in tangible, practical ways — for example, to get a job, chum with others, court our girlfriend/boyfriend, and so forth.

The downside is that we can also repeat a negative behaviour; such patterning of behaviour out of our Orthodoxy is the basis for the insight by the ancient lyric poet, Horace, who said:

**You can take a pitchfork to human nature,
but it will always come back.**

This quote is attested to by the field of psychiatry, which does NOT know how to change Human Nature. All psychiatry can do is temporise human problems through the use of drugs. This myopic approach has underpinned the explosion of pharmaceutical companies into multibillion-dollar enterprises.

Contrary to what Horace and the field of psychiatry have proposed, this book shows how it is possible to change Human Nature and cure people of their chronic smoking, alcoholism, depression, anxiety, schizoid states, and so forth.

An interesting proposition? Then read on!

Forward (I)

The Chongs' latest book is a definitive summary of how it is possible "to change Human Nature and [actually] cure people of their chronic smoking, alcoholism, depression, anxiety, schizoid states, and so forth." It is magnificent, profound beyond words, and a joy to read. It is peppered with humour throughout, which serves to break up the encyclopaedia of critical new information into a brilliant yet simple package. These pages contain a genuine revolution in thought and understanding so radical that it can change the world of counselling and psychology. The authors' personal and humorous style makes this book eminently readable and enjoyable. Dr. Chong and wife, Jennifer, are geniuses. Their breakthrough perspective gives us tools for regaining sovereignty over our lives.

The simple question, "Is it possible to change?" leads Dennis and Jennifer to explore change and "the change of change." When reading this book, you will discover how we are a system and abide in systems that are governed by organizational hierarchies. You will discover the philosophy, language, and logic of those systems. How are we influenced by acting "as if" or "if this, then that"? You will discover "how-one-knows-to-be" and "how-one-KNOWS-TO-KNOW-to-be."

The Chongs' new field of study is called Epiepistemology, or E^{epi}. We learn what makes a good question and how to ask a good question. We learn that opinions are not — and can never be — facts. We learn why "why?" is not a question for getting knowledge and what we actually get from asking "why?"

For those of us who have once said, "I've had this problem all my life," there is hope. We can change our Human Nature so that we can say, "I no longer have that problem."

Herein, we can take Yoda's advice to Luke Skywalker: You have to unlearn, what you have learnt. In this world of chaos, Dennis and Jennifer bring clarity to our Human Nature. This work is thought provoking, insightful, and will hopefully lead people to ask better-quality questions and make better decisions.

Dennis once blessed me with a quote, which I now return to him and Jennifer: This work is "deliciously mad, maddeningly exquisite, exquisitely demanding, demandingly rigorous, rigorously challenging, and challengingly excellent!"

Scout Cloud Lee, EdD

Forward (II)

Dennis and Jennifer Chong are professional collaborators and life partners. One can only marvel at how fascinating the talk at the Chong dinner table has been and continues to be.

The full range of their exploration is astonishing. They have run a robust and highly successful medical and counselling practice for decades, leading countless clients to effective outcomes. And along the way, they've unmasked and mastered hitherto undocumented language systems, exposed the limitations of cause-effect thinking, developed workshops to share their learnings in Neuro-Semantics, and delved into the very heart of Human Nature!

Yet they've chosen not to simply rest on the laurels of their success but rather to continue documenting and publishing their accumulated wisdom.

Driven by their boundless curiosity about people, language, and human development, they bring us their latest volume, *Human Nature — Is It Possible to Change It?* Not only does it take the reader into their latest insights, but it connects those insights with the foundational material that precedes it. The book is the second part and natural follow-up to the volume *Do You Know How Another Knows to Be?*

Human Nature — Is It Possible to Change It? will delight both returning learners and those who are new to the Chongs' work.

March 2021

Gary Phillips, MA, CRSP, CHRL
    NLP Trainer, consultant, personal and executive coach

Abbreviations

Analog Contract	AC
Ancillary 14	An^{Y}14
Aristotelian System of Cause and Effect	A
Body Language	BL
Compelling Referential Experience	CRE
Epiepistemology	E^{epi}
First-Order Change	IOC
Gathering Information Module	GIM
Holarchy of Paradigms	HOPs
Human Nature	HN
Infinite Void of Empty Nothingness	IVOEN
Informal Logic	IL
Language Structure	LS
Modified Meta Model	3M
Neuro-Linguistic Programming	NLP
Neuro-Semantic Programming	NSP
Non-Aristotelian System of Relativity and Relatedness	Ã
No-Y-ian Model of Language	~YML
Ontological Equation	On^{T}Eq^{N}
Ontological Theorem	On^{T}Th^{M}
Second-Order Change	IIOC
Spoken Language	Ad^{e}
Therapeutic Algorithm	TA
Virtual Logic	VL
Virtual Philosophy	VP

Introduction

This work has its origins in three unusual questions that were put forward by certain searchers over a span of two millennia. The first two were asked by pre-Socratic philosophers in 475 BC: "How do you *know-to-be*?" and "How do you **know-to**-*know-to-be*?"

Then there was a gap of more than two thousand years, at which point a third question was put forward. It was formulated by us.

Each of these three questions had incredible consequences and yielded equally incredible insights, as outlined in the following table:

By the Ancient Greek Pre-Socratic Philosophers

Question #1	How do you *know-to-be*?
Consequence	The study of **Ontology** This then-new field of study explored the fabric of human subjective reality and, by extension, the foundations of human sentience, or our way of Being. The study of Ontology sought to discover the critical elements that constituted the structure of human subjective experience.
New Insights	1. The language of the Aristotelian System of Cause and Effect (**A**) 2. The language of the Non-Aristotelian System of Relativity and Relatedness (**Ã**) 3. The metalanguage of the Modified Meta Model (**3M**)

| | 4. The No-Y-ian Model of Language (~**YML**) |
| | 5. The language of Informal Logic (**IL**) discovered by formal logicians and linguists and not us |

Also by the Ancient Greek Pre-Socratic Philosophers

Question #2	How do you **know-to-*know-to-be***?
Consequence	The study of Epistemology This study asks: What is the faculty by which a person puts his ontology to use?
New Insights	To express oneself in order to get a job, link with others, seek a mate, create a new business, and so forth.

The third question builds on the first two, and it was, for us, a challenging discovery to-know-to-ask-it.[1] It is as follows:

Our Challenging Discovery

Question #3	Do you **KNOW** how another **knows-to-*know-to-be***?
Consequence	The study of **Epiepistemology**, also known as Neuro-Semantic Programming™ (NSP) To know how to ask specific questions and get the answer allows you to know how the

---

[1] It was a challenging discovery to-know-to-ask-it because, by our cognitive logic, it was a question that in all probability no one could ever answer. Put simply, the question appeared to be a waste of time. However, as we probed the matter, we discovered that it was, in fact, possible to get the answers.

	other knows-to-be. With the answer, one would be able to understand the other, whether in therapeutic or pragmatic contexts or applications.
Results	From this incredible discovery came the knowledge that **Therapeutic Algorithms (TAs)** can address all forms of mental ill health.

In pragmatic terms, to **KNOW** how another **knows-to-**know-to-be is equivalent to saying, when one marvels about another,

My, you really know this person inside out!
or
You have such a thorough grasp of this person.

What is implied is that a human being is ahead of the curve of the other. And the field of Epiepistemology is the study of how to *truly know their thinking*; because of this, by extension, one can know their future-oriented motives, moves, plans, intentions, aims, targets, goals, ambitions, wants, and desires.

The alternative is to live forever in the dark abyss of never knowing about the person you are with. We believe that this is known as the *bliss of ignorance*. We are not sure that this is the healthiest way to live.

Neuro-Semantic Programming v. Psychiatry

The effect of asking this third question has been to unlock a new set of possibilities for addressing mental ill health. Unlike the psychiatric establishment, which specialises in drugging patients to alleviate suffering, often without getting to know them as human beings, Neuro-Semantic Programming addresses the whole person and their wider context. Rejecting quick fixes in favour of longer-term strategies and deeper knowledge, NSP engages in the careful and often highly effective work of studying each person and their suffering in light of social context, language, and a host of other attributes that shape our conscious and unconscious ways of knowing and being in the world.

If you have acquired the skill to truly know the person, through NSP, you are then in a position to better understand and help them. The answer to the question of how each person knows-to-be is already in the Being of each person, and he or she knows it *unconsciously.* Knowing and then helping another begins with asking good questions. A good question is one that is calibrated to address a patient's symptoms or mental ill health so that the question itself has the power to unlock a cure. When you ask the correct question of a person, they will automatically know how to answer it. The odd thing is, they will have no awareness of having revealed anything of themself to you because the knowledge of how they know-to-be is naturally an integral part of each person.

These dynamics can be explained by way of a simple example. None of us, as we sit down to breakfast or settle into our desk chair at work, gives much conscious thought to the weight of our bum on the seat. We just sit down without thinking about it. Yet, unconsciously, we know the weight of our bum. Therefore, if you were to ask someone, "How does your bum feel right now on your seat?" he or she would have no difficulty giving you the answer.

Who lives with a mindful awareness of their left fifth toe? If you ask someone, "How is your left fifth toe feeling at this moment?" they will answer automatically by telling you it's fine. In the next instant, they will have forgotten about it. But the knowledge is there — with or without conscious awareness.

Therapeutic Algorithms

In tandem with asking good questions, our therapeutic methods rely on algorithms. A Therapeutic Algorithm (TA) is a manoeuvre or a set of manoeuvres designed to effect a cure. The first time we encountered this approach, it was in the context of an incredible cure for aerophobia, the fear of flying. Sometime in the late 1970s, the cost of air travel came down, and flying became more accessible. Suddenly, vast numbers of people who could never afford to fly on airplanes found that it was within their grasp. As a result, thousands of people learned that they had a fear of flying. The offices of family medical physicians and psychiatrists were inundated with these patients. No one had a cure for it. Psychiatry eventually came up with a therapy called desensitization. It cost a lot of money and tended not to work.

Then one day, the field study of Neuro-Linguistic Programming (NLP), under the aegis of Richard Bandler and John Grinder, found the cure. They called their manoeuvre a Therapeutic Algorithm and named it the Flying Phobia Cure. NLP is the study of language in relation to how we think. In those early days, the treatment took an hour. With time, certain members of the NLP community brought that figure down to six minutes. This led to it being called the Six-Minute Flying Phobia Cure. It was so effective that you almost never hear of anyone with aerophobia nowadays. Thanks to Bandler and Grinder and others who refined the technique, anyone who has it can be cured quickly.

Therapeutic Algorithms offer a systematic and highly effective set of tools for addressing a wide variety of problems. At its most basic level, a TA is a set of prescribed steps that are either applied to the client by a therapist or performed by the client on themself. When it is done correctly, the person will be cured of the problem.

The reader will note that we have been talking about a *cure* for aerophobia. This brings us to an important matter. What does it mean to say that one can cure a mental disorder? This question is one of the central concerns of the book and receives special attention in Chapter XII. However, to answer this question, we must first consider how thinking about different levels of change within social groups and individuals can occur.

Watzlawick, Weakland, and Fisch (1974) give the example of a person having a nightmare. In a nightmare, a person can often do many things, including "run, hide, fight, scream," but can't end the nightmare. The only way out of a dream is by waking, which involves changing from one state to another. The authors refer to the first type of change as a First-Order Change (IOC), whereas the movement from one state to another (from sleeping to waking, for example) is referred to as a Second-Order Change (IIOC).

A framework for these inquiries can be found in their 1974 book *CHANGE: Principles of Problem Formation and Problem Resolution*. The aforementioned authors distinguish between two types of change: one inside the system, which the authors call Group Theory; and another that changes the system itself, which the authors call the Theory of Logical Types. Group Theory refers to "a framework for thinking about the kind of change that can occur *within a system* that itself stays invariant," and gives us "a frame for considering the relationship between member and class and the peculiar metamorphosis which is in the nature of shifts from one logical level to the next higher." It also distinguishes between two different types of change: "one that occurs within a given system which itself remains unchanged [IOC], and *one whose occurrence changes the system itself* [IIOC]" (p. 10, emphasis ours).

The result of their thinking was that an IIOC is a "*change of change* — the very phenomenon whose existence Aristotle denied so categorically" (p. 11). Put simply, when you are in one system, its rules of operation will determine its unique changes. Such changes in the system are examples of First-Order Change. In the case cited above, the brain neurology of sleep is a system. All the nightmares experienced are IOCs. This includes any attempts by the dreamer to get out of the dream while still sleeping. However, as soon as the dreamer wakes up and the dream ends, then we're in the territory of Second-Order Change. When the brain switches over to the neurology for human wakefulness, then all its changes relative to the neurology of sleeping fall into the category of Second-Order Change.

A person's neurology of Being, or baseline neurological state, is normal for that person, and all changes that flow from it would be examples of IOC. Such changes are also ontological. However, when the neurology of Being becomes abnormal and manifests, such as that of a person with chronic depression or schizophrenia, those would be examples of IIOC. In therapy, in this instance, the central question is one of how to bring Second-Order Change back to First-Order Change. Doing so would guide a person toward a more meaningful future, out of a negative state to a more positive one, which would be considered a cure.

Changes of Action through a Change in Ontology

A real-world (or a reality-TV-world) example of how this is done can be found in the TV series, *Restaurant Impossible.* In each episode, the show's host, Chef Robert Irvine, has forty-eight hours to rescue a failing restaurant from bankruptcy. In almost every case, we can see that the restaurant got into trouble because of the people involved. The failures of each business enterprise are the result of human error and, indeed, flawed Human Nature, at every level, from the owner(s) to the serving staff at the front of house and the kitchen staff at the back.

At the core of his success is Chef Irvine's ability to bring about a change from a flawed IIOC back to an IOC. He takes restaurant owners whose businesses are about to sink and finds a way to turn them around. Yes, this is a reality TV show. Even so, we have been consistently impressed by Chef Irvine's gifts as an amateur therapist who seems to know, instinctively, how to help the show's participants rescue their own businesses.

When we first viewed this series, what Chef Irvine was doing seemed so simple, normal, and natural, we did not realise that what he was doing was, in fact, stunning, wonderful, and incredible.

We momentarily forgot our own adaptation to the ancient lyric poet's maxim:

> **You can take a pitchfork to human nature,**
> **but it will always come back.**

Put simply, from ancient times, it was already recognised that to change Human Nature, the neurology of Being, is impossible. This is something that orthodox conventional psychiatry has long recognised. However, life's rule is:

**For a generalization to be valid,
there must be exceptions.**

Chef Irvine is most certainly a wonder and an extraordinary exception to the rule of the ancient lyric poet. He asks good questions of his participants and gets them to change their behaviour so that their businesses go from failing to flourishing.

We now know that the phenomenon of IIOC back to IOC can also be reversed. Then it is IOC to IIOC; and, significantly, this can happen normally in life. When this happens, there is a volte-face in the person's way of life.

You may know of such an event happening to a relative, friend (or friend of a friend), or colleague, or you may have seen a case reported on TV or in a newspaper. At this instant, we can recall two cases. The first, which came to us via YouTube, concerned a Parisian who was famous in the world of finance. One day he walked out of his job and opened a steak-and-frites restaurant in Paris. Today, the line-up to eat at his restaurant goes from the door to the end of the block. The second was from the *National Enquirer* — not a highly credentialed news outlet but one that sometimes coughs up an interesting example. In it we read the case of a Carmelite nun who renounced her order, her vows, and her faith to become one of Los Angeles's top ladies of the night. Each of these cases indicates a Second-Order Change in their lives.

Milton H. Erickson

Other examples of going from IIOC to IOC and IOC to IIOC can be found in the work of famed clinicians such as Milton Erickson, MD;

his students; and Virginia Satir. They achieved their results by applying what Neuro-Linguistic Programming (NLP) and Epiepistemology (NSP) now recognise as Therapeutic Algorithms. In contradistinction to NLP, NSP is the study of semantics behind the language (i.e., the *meaning* of language) and is our theoretical extension of NLP. NSP has extracted A (Cause and Effect) from NLP and re-embedded NLP in a new language system of $\tilde{A}$ (relativity and relatedness). Rather than analyse how one thinks (alone), NSP looks to *who* we are and *how* we know-to-know-to-be who we are.

We will cite here an example of a TA developed by Milton Erickson. It concerned a couple who were prone to nocturnal enuresis, or bed wetting. Following the happiness of the wedding and the bliss of their first nuptial night together, they were shocked to find themselves waking up in a wet bed. Neither had informed the other of their problem. The result was that each took silent responsibility for the event. Each did everything they could to assure the dignity of the other. It was only further on in their marriage that they discovered that they were both responsible for the wet bed.

They were now before Erickson, stuck in their Human Natures of bed wetting. At the second consultation, he exacted a promise from them that they would carry out the treatment he prescribed. They each genuinely gave their promise that they would.

This was the treatment. Each night before bed, they were to follow their usual routine of saying their nightly prayers. Then they were to pull back the bed sheets, urinate on the bed, and go to sleep. They were to return and report in a week.

When they returned, they reported that they had stopped wetting the bed. The treatment had guided them away from a warped Human Nature to a healthier one, wherein a bed was no longer an acceptable place to urinate. Erickson discusses the treatment in *Advanced Techniques of Hypnosis and Therapy* (pp. 410–412).

Epiepistemology gives us many other examples of cures brought about by the application of TAs. There is a class of people who, by their Human Nature, are hair pullers. The name for this condition is trichotillomania. Psychiatry considers this condition incurable. A person came to us suffering from trichotillomania. I (Dennis) exacted from her a promise that she would do exactly as prescribed and follow to the letter the treatment I would put to her. Satisfied that she would carry out my directions, I then told her to do the following:

> Continue with a free heart to pull your hair, but each time you do so, you must note when you do it. At the end of the day, you will have the record of the number of times you pulled your hair; thereafter, pull two more than the times you pulled your hair (i.e., if it was three times, go to your bathroom mirror and pull out five hairs). I would like you to report in one week.

When she returned, she reported that she had stopped pulling her hair.

There is, today (2021), at the time of writing, an emergent field of study regarding (1) where a mental disorder is located in the neurology of Being, (2) what the structure of a mental disorder is, and (3) the invention or creation of the TA for the diagnosis.

Following on this structure, we have added to the TA an extraction of a promise from the client, which we call an Analog Contract (AC). Although this is not a feature of every TA, it is a feature in NSP that a TA has an AC to have proven effectiveness; and for that, we believe AC deserves its own term.

In this book, we elaborate on the ideas underpinning Neuro-Semantic Programming and the many ways TAs and good questions can be brought to bear on seemingly incurable forms of mental ill health. We take you through the foundations of the field, explain how it differs from the fields of psychiatry and NLP, and support our argument that, with careful attention to the human being in their social and linguistic contexts, Human Nature can be changed, and in the process, mental ill health can be cured.

Chapter I

Systems in A and $\bar{A}$

In this chapter, we dig into some of the conceptual foundations of Epistemology and define some of the terms and concepts that you will encounter throughout this book. (Further definitions of the other specialised language related to these inquiries can be found in the glossary).

This chapter begins by elaborating on basic *systems*, including those related to philosophy, language, and logic. We also explore three additional language systems: a more congruent and productive system of $\bar{A}$; the metalanguage of the Modified Meta Model, 3M; and the No-Y-ian Model of Language, ~YML. A variety of philosophical, mathematical, and ontological models and systems are considered to help us differentiate the Blame Frame from the Freedom Frame. Our work in Epiepistemology, or NSP, is situated in the Freedom Frame.

Respectfully, we surmise that there might be certain critical semantic items that you may not be familiar with. Therefore, in this chapter, we will go over them with you. The purpose is to clarify and help you to go into the flow of your reading of this work. If you are already familiar with a term, you may skip over it.

Systems

Systems include the following characteristics:

1. A system is a hierarchical organization governed by rules. At each level of the hierarchy is a supervising authority. Thus, in a flight from Vancouver to Singapore, the captain is the number-one authority. In the flight cabin, it is the chief steward. In the galley for first-class passengers, the head flight attendant is the boss.

2. As all systems are hierarchical, they have sub-systems, sub-sub-systems, and so forth.

3. We are all in systems. When you were growing up, you did so in your unique family system.

4. There are countless systems, each one distinct. Thus, when you are in an airplane you are in the system of that flight. The system in a McDonald's restaurant is not the same as in a Japanese Teppanyaki restaurant.

5. When we are in a system, our actions accord with the implicate grammar of the system. Many of us have had incredible fun at a pub with our friends. However, such pub behaviours will not do during a Sunday church service.

6. All systems have their philosophy. The Lutheran religion has its philosophy. In the system of Western civilisation, Canada has its model of Western philosophy. In the constitution of Singapore, English is declared to be one of Singapore's national languages. For this, English has functionally become the *lingua franca* of Singapore. So, it has Western civilisation too — but Singapore-style.

7. The philosophy of a system is a Virtual Philosophy (VP), by virtue of the fact that we live unconsciously within it. We internalise the rules of the society we live in to such an extent that these rules become second nature and simply run in the background within us.

8. All systems have logic.

9. By analogy to VP, its logic is therefore a Virtual Logic (VL).

10. All VL systems have languages, verbal and non-verbal. Visit rural Japan and rural England, and you will see differences in

their native, automatic Body Language (BL). If you compare their national dances, they will be different.

The Philosophy, Language, and Logic of Virtual Systems

Earlier, we listed five distinct language systems: A, Ā, 3M, ~YML, and IL. Awareness of these five language systems is taught in the Freedom Seminars and in later chapters of this book.

From the time we were born, our parents instilled into us their spoken or native language (e.g., English) within the constraints of the Language Structures (LSs) of the Aristotelian System of Cause and Effect (A). We all use the different forms of Informal Logic (IL) to convey our arguments in life. When the authors went to school, we were already competent speakers of English and culturally trained in recognizing and deploying our language, philosophy, and logic within the semantic boundaries of A and IL. Such is true for all language systems (Spanish, German, etc.) with the exception of the Hopi language.

What few people realise is that it is by the power of A and IL that we are propelled into the trajectory and the orbit of our lives (constrained within our own unique and shared environment). In 2023, Jeff Bezos is one of the world's richest men by virtue of the unique quality of his grasp and deployment of Cause and Effect and Informal Logic and because of the unique character of his Human Nature (HN). Similarly, by the unique quality of his A and IL and the unique character of his HN, you will find a homeless man living on a street in San Francisco.

The Aristotelian System of Cause and Effect produces one set of cultural, linguistic, and philosophical tendencies that have been dominant in many cultures for centuries. We have argued that Cause and Effect keeps people in a Blame Frame, in part by prioritizing the question of *why* a given thing happens or *why* a person takes a given action. Asking *why* automatically puts the listener on the defensive by implying that they must justify their thoughts or actions. But there are alternatives. In our epistemological shift away from the structures of Cause and Effect, we focus on the benefits of taking on other language systems and their more freeing philosophies. In this book, we'll ask you to consider the consequences for you, at this time in your life, of adding to your mastery of the languages of A and IL a mastery of the following:

- the languages of the Non-Aristotelian System of Relativity and Relatedness, $\bar{A}$
- the metalanguage of the Modified Meta Model, 3M
- the No-Y-ian Model of Language, ~YML

If you had mastery over the three language systems listed above, their Virtual Philosophy would automatically be part of you. If you master the grammar of the English language and you live or have lived in London, England, you will have a British VP, albeit with some distinctions and variations based upon your An^Y14 (see Chapter II). If you move from England to California, you will, over time, exhibit a hybrid VP that combines aspects of British and Californian ways of Being in the world. If you live in Beijing and master Mandarin, you have its Virtual Philosophy automatically. The VP automatically becomes part of you because it is carried in the language and subsequent culture.

How do we know that, if you master a language, you will automatically have its VP and, by extension, its logic and its psychological attitude of life? I (Dennis) was born in Kuala Lumpur, Malaysia. Until the age of fourteen, I spoke English, but I could also speak Cantonese and a smattering of Malay. In me was my evolving and maturing Virtual Philosophy, logic, and psychological attitude. Then I was sent to a private boarding school run by Jesuits. I studied Medicine at the University of Leeds and had a Family Medical Practice in Yorkshire, UK. I came to Canada and joined a Family Medical Practice in Perth County, Ontario, and then worked in hypnosis and therapy in Oakville, Ontario. I am now eighty-three. I can witness that my core Being from the age of fourteen in Malaysia morphed into its final form in 1999, when I was sixty-three years old.

If our implicit proposition is accurate, then, if you think about how you have developed, evolved, and morphed over the years, you will recognise the great milestones you went through in your life. With them, if you allow yourself to be aware, you will recognise how your core Being changed.

Each version of your core Being is part of your Human Nature at that time in your life.

The Hierarchy of Language in Human Communication

Human communication follows a hierarchy that is embedded in the structure of language. The first and simplest level includes a single oral utterance that may or may not be an accepted word with a definition attached. Word-sounds — like *Ouch! Oh! Nah! Oooh! Heck!* or *Boo!* — carry a simple, expressive meaning and can bring across a lot of information all at once.

Slightly higher in the hierarchy are single words — actual words with definitions attached — that appear often in interpersonal situations, such as when an action needs to be completed or when one speaker seeks to inform, question, or answer another speaker. Single words — like *Yes, No, When? Where? How? Go! Out! Faster!* — convey a lot of information quickly and provide the linguistic glue for countless situations in every human society.

Next in the hierarchy are phrases, such as *Surely not? Wonderfully amazing! Utterly befuddling. What cost?! Definitely NOT! Gotcha! Where in hell? In heaven's name!* Phrases combine meaning sets into more complex wholes and can veer into metaphor, as happens with idioms, like *Until the cows come home* or *It's a dog-eat-dog world.*

Another type of phrase implies a sort of contract between speakers and can enact a promise — or block the possibility of a promise — in the act of speaking. Thus, when we say things like *OK, I'll do it* or *No! I won't* or *Go to hell* or *God be praised* or *Be civil*, we're using language to cement (or break down) social relationships.

Of course, we can also communicate using longer and more complex sentences. Such sentences convey information and can mix and match the functions of language that have already been alluded to, allowing speakers to make or break promises, convey information and emotion, give and get answers, and fulfil higher-order functions, like strengthening or weakening human bonds.

One interesting facet of language is that we communicate by Language Structures (LSs). A Language Structure is the name of a file for a semantic topic that contains all possible vocabulary, slangs, and sentences that pertain to it. An example would be Yorkshire pudding. If you are familiar with it, you may have your version of a recipe for it. You may also have other LS items in your LS file for Yorkshire pudding, including a phrase that your parents used when they served it at home or the slang term for it that you and your fellow students used whenever a dull version of it was served at school or a scene from a British novel — probably something by Dickens — that included Yorkshire pudding. Your Language Structure will be filled with the words, slang, sentences, and other associations that have become attached to Yorkshire pudding in your lived experience. This could be as simple as one recipe or as complex as a nest of literary and social associations. Moreover, the more complex the originating object, the larger the LS file. While your LS file for Yorkshire pudding might contain one recipe, your LS file for the Holy Trinity could include an indefinite number of volumes (of contrasting beliefs).

The Philosophy of 'As if'

In his book *The Philosophy of 'As if,'* Hans Vaihinger showed that, in a significant and substantial way, we all live the life of *as if*. Our take on his classic example is that I, as a human being and citizen of Canada, **never signed any document** in which I agreed to abide by the laws that have been enacted, are being enacted, and will be enacted by the Parliament of Canada — and neither has any other citizen, from the day of the inception of Canada as a nation to today.

If this is so, how is it that we (the authors) as Canadian citizens live in obedience to all laws that are in the statutes of the Canadian Parliament? We do so because, as Hans Vaihinger showed, *it is as if* we had all, in fact, signed this document. Upon this **AS IF** we are bound to obey all legally enacted Canadian laws. Wow! It is quite some fantasy! But it is a semantically well-formed fantasy, with all the features of **the REAL**. It also has all the power of the state and its legal system to enforce it. It is, therefore, an amazing fact of life that there are co-citizens who actually live in denial of this.

Every Philosophy Has Its Unique Language

The philosophy of a civilisation holds the logic of the people of that civilisation, and this logic is carried and contained in its language. And from this logic unfurls the unique patterns of linguistic behaviour associated with that civilisation; such patterns determine our civil and social behaviours.

Now, the structure of society is hierarchical. If you are in its upper echelons, your patterns and style of linguistic, civil, and social behaviour will not be the same as those in the lower orders. Moreover, within these echelons, further distinctions flow from the cues and habits of one's environment.

Consider the example of a high-priced criminal lawyer who somehow ends up at a conference for neurosurgeons at the Delta Inn in Toronto. He or she would probably miss all sorts of social cues and be at a loss for how to behave or what to say. And the same fate would await a top neurosurgeon who somehow ends up at a conference for international lawyers at the Plaza Hotel in New York. Although they are both professionals, they will be fish out of water because their respective language systems are uniquely different from each other. Think of how it would be for you to be a registrant at a one-day annual conference of the Plumbers Association of Southern Ontario. Unless you are a plumber, would you understand what you were hearing? Would you feel comfortable or out of place?

Modus Ponens

Later, we devote a chapter to the subject of modus ponens. Latin for "method of affirming," modus ponens is a deductive argument form and a rule of inference that speaks to the value between two variables and is used to draw logical conclusions. It can be summarised as follows: P implies Q. P is true. Therefore, Q must also be true.

At its briefest, it says,

If this, **then** that.

Thus, in the domain of human emotions and action,

If you persist in your dismissive attitude toward him, **then** all you will get will be enmity and resentment.
If her husband gets angry, **then** she will collapse helplessly.
If her precious darling cries, **then** she always gives in.
If you had the money, **then** you could buy the two-million-dollar car.
If you study well and do your homework with diligence, **then** you will pass.

The above five examples show that *structurally* we normally think this way. Closely related to the modus ponens is the modus tollens. In propositional logic, modus tollens (Latin for "method of removing by taking away") is a deductive argument form and a rule of inference. Modus tollens takes the form of "If P, then Q. Not Q. Therefore, not P." It is an application of the general truth that if a statement is true, then so is its contrapositive. An example of a modus tollens is studying [Q] and passing [P]:

If you do *not* do your studies or homework [~Q], **then** you will fail [~P].

Very few grasp the pivotal role played by the modus ponens in mathematics. Take this simple example, which every grade school student is taught:

$$C = 2\pi r$$

What is this equation saying? It is saying that, if the value of the radius (r) is multiplied by 2π, you will have the value of the circumference (C).

In a right-angle triangle, ABC, you will remember the theorem of Pythagoras:

$$AC^2 = AB^2 + BC^2$$

What is the theorem saying? That the square of the hypotenuse of a right-angle triangle is equal to the sum of the squares of the other two sides. From these two examples, because of the equals sign, you have a modus ponens. *If* you know the values of the variables on the right side of an equation, when you tote them up, *then* you get the value of the left side of the equation, and vice versa. The philosophy of mathematics — specifically, that equality *is* a modus ponens — is hardly ever discussed or overtly shown, even in higher mathematics.

Body Language (BL)

Briefly, BL has nine components to it and is empowered by the meta function;[2] the meta function is our ability to abstract, thereby think, *about* it. These categories are as follows: (1) opinions, (2) interpretations, (3) views, (4) ideas, (5) evaluations, (6) self-evaluations, (7) judgements, (8) determinations, and (9) conclusions. As we concluded in *Do You Know How Another Knows to Be?*

---

[2] For in-depth information on the meta function, please refer to our earlier work, *Do You Know How Another Knows to Be?*, page 11.

As a man thinketh in his heart, so is he!

Body Language also has its own philosophy. This subject will be dealt with in Chapter VIII.

Ontology

It was the pre-Socratic Greek philosophers who first began to explore the question "How does a person *know-to-be*?"

By this simple question, they were in fact attempting to find out the following:

- What is the fabric of human subjective reality?
- What generates it?
- What are the elements that constitute its structure?
- Whatever it is, how does it know to produce the fabric to fit the semantic context that the person is in?

They (Parmenides et alia) named their field of study Ontology, which later became one of the critical, overarching subjects of psychiatric research. Our work of Neuro-Semantic Programming (NSP) further advances this genealogical lineage. We argue that a person's ontology, or their way of Being, is at the crux of any problem state that needs to change.

Epistemology

For the ancient Greek philosophers, to have just the faculty of ontology, or *to-know-to-be*, was insufficient. One had

TO-KNOW-*to-know-to-be*.

By this second faculty, one who *knows-to-know-to-be* is one who can and will express their ontology to get a job to earn a living, to affiliate with others, to do military service, to find a spouse, and so forth. Epistemology was a further extension along the genealogical track of our development and research.

Epiepistemology

In our forty-one years of dedicated inquiry, search, research, examination, exploration into "how-one-*knows-to-be*," and "how-one-**KNOWS-TO**-*know-to-be*," we came to the logical moment of wondering whether we could ever **"KNOW**-how-(another)-**KNOWS-TO**-*know-to-be*."

To have this faculty would be of great value to any healing tradition as one would be aware of another person's Stuck State; they would then be in a position to unravel a person's problem and cure them of their semantically ill-formed state.

This kind of advancement would spell the end of drudgery and chemicalization of human beings within Stuck States. This book demonstrates, in careful detail, how it is possible to *know-how-another-knows-to-know-to-be* and shows how this therapeutic advantage can be leveraged to help people get out of Stuck States.

This is a new field of study. Initially we just knew to name it Neuro-Semantic Programming™ (NSP). We thank Roland Roye Fraser for getting the trademark for us.

However, it was the ancient pre-Socratic philosophers who signposted us to NSP. It dawned on us that we had a deep desire to honour and acknowledge them. In their honour, the name of this new field of study has to be

Epiepistemology (E^{epi}).

Chapter II

HOPs and An^{Y}14

What Are the Holarchy of Paradigms (HOPs)?

We all use blueprints of life to understand ourselves, others, and the world we live in. Formally, these blueprints are known as our semantic paradigms, which we have abbreviated to *paradigms* in usage.

Think about this. Our paradigm of significance — and perhaps that of many of our readers — is Western civilisation. We, Jennifer and Dennis, are the products of Western civilisation, and, since you are reading this, it's possible that you are too (though you may not be, in which case, the paradigms we're discussing will differ from your own). Intellectually, between us there are differences. For example, Jennifer subscribes fiercely to the place of feminism, whereas I am not as fierce on the subject as she is.

You can instantly grasp that someone born in Osaka is a product of a different civilization — a Japanese civilisation. Do we have to list the differences, in subtleties and nuances of Body Language, between a person born in Osaka and someone born in Canada?

There are three categories of paradigms:

1. Meta-Paradigm
2. General Paradigms
3. Specific Paradigms

These categories come together to form a unity, which we have called the Holarchy of Paradigms:

Holarchy of Paradigms - HOPs

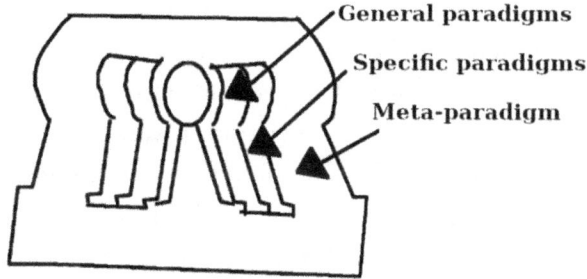

General paradigms
Specific paradigms
Meta-paradigm

At first, they were named the Hierarchy of Paradigms. However, from the work of Arthur Koestler, we recognised that each paradigm is a *whole*. Since we are dealing with wholes within wholes, we decided to rename this unity the Holarchy of Paradigms (HOPs). The term *holarchy* was coined by Koestler in his 1967 book *The Ghost in the Machine*. It refers to a type of hierarchy that describes the relationship between parts and wholes (a whole/part) rather than the relative value of different levels within a part or a whole. Whereas a hierarchy has an absolute top and bottom, and different values are almost always assigned to those positions, the relationship between holons in a holarchy can be described with terms like "in and out" instead of "up and down" or "left and right."

There are also sub-systems within sub-systems of language. Apart from being a large city in England, London is also an LS because embedded in the proper noun is a vast number of subsets of an LS, or what we can call a sub-LS. We will cite five examples of these smaller sets within sets, as follows:

1. Hyde Park
2. the London Underground
3. Buckingham Palace

4.   King's College

5.   London's recycling water system

For each of these sub-LSs, there are volumes upon volumes of books written about them. Each place has a language system as it relates to who we are. In the hierarchy of language, the highest level consists of exchanges between sub-LSs and sub-sub-LSs. This is how it is that if I (Dennis) were to register to attend the annual conference of the Toronto Plumbers Association, I would be totally bored and lost. Not knowing much about plumbing and not being in the habit of communicating with plumbers and not knowing how plumbers communicate, I lack most of the necessary sub-LSs and sub-sub-LSs that would allow me to fit in. I would be out of the loop.

Now consider yourself at a cocktail party where you end up as the third in a group of three. By chance, the other two are high-end antique dealers. One is from Shakespeare, Ontario; the other is from Burlington. They are so thrilled to meet each other. They relate their finds, gossip about other dealers that they know, and so forth. You will know what it feels like to be unintentionally ostracised.

Then it occurs to you that language is power. It is thus unfortunate that there is such a loss in the acquisition of vocabulary in our culture. It amazes us to conclude that, since the end of World War II, our very expensive educational system has produced a diminishing number of graduates who have evolved and developed a mastery of the English language that reflects the style and grandeur of well-spoken (e.g., Churchillian) English. In fact, there was a fierce declamation by a retired professor of optometry at the University of Waterloo that Canadian universities were admitting students who were illiterate in English. There was actually a huge brouhaha nationally (in the sense that it made the news). The so-called standards are appalling. It is of note that Dennis was ranked in the top five percent of speakers as regards breadth of vocabulary and elocution by this very UW professor.

When we turn our study to the structure of paradigms themselves, we acknowledge the existence of an overarching paradigm that we call a Meta-Paradigm. From the diagram above (page 13), our shared Meta-Paradigm determines the logic of the operations of the unity of our HOPs, which manifest in the way of our Being.

Meta-Paradigm

There are two Meta-Paradigms with only one in operation:

1. The Aristotelian System of Cause and Effect (A) consists of its own structure (outlined below) and is comprised of twelve logical levels each with its own Language Structure (LS). This system is the most general and common one at present.

2. The Non-Aristotelian System of Relativity and Relatedness ($\tilde{A}$) has its own structure equally comprised of twelve logical levels of LSs and is the alternative to A.

Below is the holarchy of the twelve logical levels of the language systems of the Aristotelian System of Cause and Effect. Feel free to consider any of the below LSs of A. We do so extensively in our previous books, where we call the LS of A the Blame Frame since each level has the element of blame. And, for each LS, there are an indefinite number of variations in a past, present, and future in a given situation. For example: "You made me angry," "You should not have done that," and "Why did you do that?" The meta result is that A is a very complex WHOLE.

The Aristotelian System

CAUSALITY

Cause and Effect

Y makes X

WHY $\Big\langle$ Reason / Explanation $\Big\rangle$ re X?

Y $\Big\langle$ SHOULD BE / SHOULD NOT BE

Y $\Big\langle$ Right / Wrong

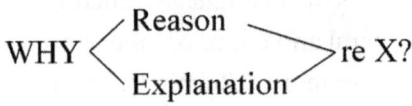

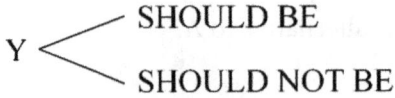

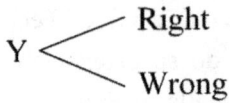

Y ——— Justification

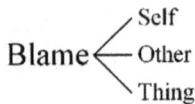

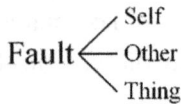

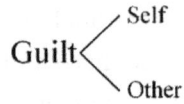

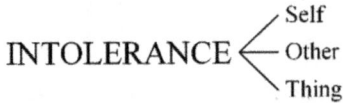

Blame $\Big\langle$ Self / Other / Thing   Fault $\Big\langle$ Self / Other / Thing   Guilt $\Big\langle$ Self / Other

INTOLERANCE $\Big\langle$ Self / Other / Thing

SELF-IMPORTANCE & PRIDE

AVOID ALL SELF-RESPONSIBILITY

MAD, MAD, MAD, MAD, MAD WORLD

If you compare and contrast the Language Structures of the Aristotelian System (A) and the Non-Aristotelian System (Ã), it will be obvious that those of Ã are *accurate to the structures of the reality we live in.* A key finding of cosmology is that our entire universe is *mathematical.* This being so, it must follow that the operations and phenomena of this universe are, at their pivot, the modus ponens of Formal Logic.

Now consider the language systems of Cause and Effect. By its structure, it does not fit what is actual to the mathematics of our reality. To take one example, we can explore the LS of the word *should.* As a word, *should* speaks to our *expectations* and, by logical extension, to our *entitlements.* The question is this: In a reality that we all know is *improbable* and *uncertain,* how on Earth is it logical to have *expectations* and *entitlements*?

You will have much fun, shock, and amusement when you work out the bewildering, illogical nonsense that is embedded in the other LSs of A. When you do so, you will, with some concern, realise that you are now in the cruel entrapment of *not being able* to use the LSs of A in your daily communication; you are now embarking on a shift from communication based on *justification* to communication based on *information.* The alternative Ã frame (see next page) is known as the Freedom Frame and uses the languages of relativity and mathematics. Information based upon the Freedom Frame is more accurate.

The Non-Aristotelian System

Relativity & Relatedness

Cybernetics & Geometrodynamics

Y = function of X

How, Who, What, When, Where, Which, Whose

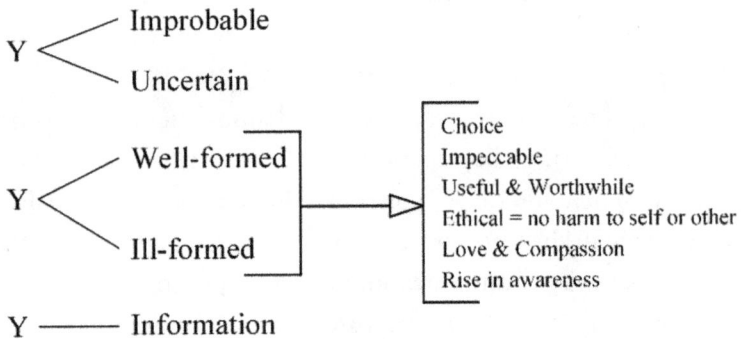

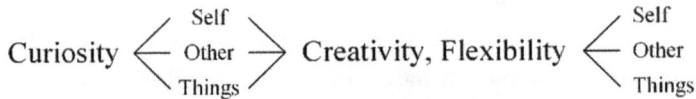

$$Y < \begin{array}{l} \text{Improbable} \\ \text{Uncertain} \end{array}$$

$$Y < \begin{array}{l} \text{Well-formed} \\ \text{Ill-formed} \end{array} \longrightarrow \begin{array}{l} \text{Choice} \\ \text{Impeccable} \\ \text{Useful \& Worthwhile} \\ \text{Ethical = no harm to self or other} \\ \text{Love \& Compassion} \\ \text{Rise in awareness} \end{array}$$

Y ——— Information

$$\text{Curiosity} \xleftarrow{} \begin{array}{l} \text{Self} \\ \text{Other} \\ \text{Things} \end{array} \xrightarrow{} \text{Creativity, Flexibility} \xleftarrow{} \begin{array}{l} \text{Self} \\ \text{Other} \\ \text{Things} \end{array}$$

Respect & Fearlessness

Self-worth & Humility

Accept all self-responsibility

Einstein's Universe

You are free to not take our advice and to stay within the Blame Frame. However, we owe it to you as the discoverers of the LSs of A and Ã to offer you the advice that flows from these discoveries. The Freedom Seminar we pioneered opens the door to take you out of the linguistic prison of the Aristotelian System.

General Paradigms

The following are the General Paradigms:

Race & History	Clan/Tribe & History	Family & History
Language & History	Dialect & History	Education System
Politics & History	History	Mathematics
Statistics	Economics & History	Commerce/Trade
Geography	Science	Military & History
Customs	Traditions	Legends

The principal function of the General Paradigms is to create the identity of personhood and nationhood and to generate the binding loyalties that each member of the collective owes to each other. In other words, the General Paradigms are the ones we share with everyone. These bonds are fractured under conditions of civil war when conflict arises over religious opinions, dynastic succession, and political or economic differences.

Thus, in the history of the British nation, except in

1. its civil war, the War of the Roses,
2. the political differences regarding the suzerainty between the Crown and Parliament, and
3. religious differences (e.g., between extremist Islamism and Christianity at the beginning of the twenty-first century),

we have not seen native-born Britons set out to kill other Britons en masse. Then, in London, on July 7, 2005 (usually referred to as 7/7), three native-born Brits and one Jamaican-born set out to bomb other Brits. While we leave it to the reader to research the specifics of these attacks, the salient point here is that the 7/7 London bombings reveal the fractures that can exist within a society.

Specific Paradigms

The list of possible Specific Paradigms is vast. We will offer five examples of statements that arise out of Specific Paradigms. From the intellectual flavour of these statements, we think you can surmise what the rest could be:

"All politicians are crooks."

"Lawyers are bottom feeders."

"Women do not like me."

"I am not sure whether I can make it in life."

"People must be charitable and generous."

From a structural point of view, most Specific Paradigms are

- functions of modal operators[3] and their concordant *expectations* and *entitlements*
- opinions, usually negative, about self or others
- negative inferences or conclusions about self or others

The Meta-Paradigm, General Paradigms, and Specific Paradigms form a unity that we originally named the Hierarchy of Paradigms. However, as mentioned, Arthur Koestler's writing guided us to see

---

[3] **modal operators** were once known as the *imperatives* of the English language. They included such words as *should, must, mandatory, required,* and so forth. Embedded in all imperatives are expectations and entitlements. Given that we live in a reality of the unknown, in which nothing is guaranteed, it makes no sense to nurse expectations or a sense of entitlement. Because of *should,* can you give up expecting ... ever? Here we see the lack of logic and deficiencies of the A system as untrue to fact. A strict adherence to *should* — when unfulfilled — may lead to disappointment, anger, bitterness, depression, and resentment. These emotions are more than enough to trip you into the abyss of the Dark Side of the Force.

that every paradigm is a *whole/part*. For this we changed the cluster of Meta-Paradigm, General Paradigms, and Specific Paradigms to the Holarchy of Paradigms (HOPs).

What Are the Ancillary 14 (An^{Y}14)?

They comprise the following:

Default Assumptions	Presuppositions	Assumptions
Beliefs	Opinions	Morality
Ethics	Metrics	Standards
Criteria	Biases	Prejudices
Customs	Traditions	

What we then discovered was this:

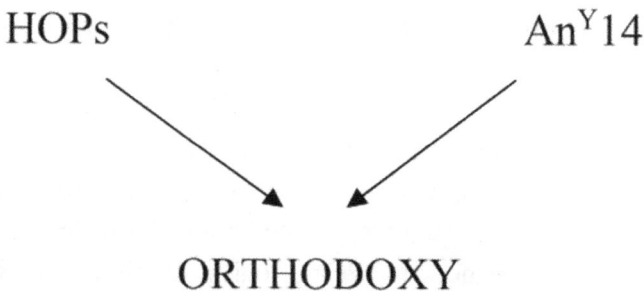

HOPs   An^{Y}14

ORTHODOXY

Human Nature unfolds from Orthodoxy. It unfolds by virtue of our actions-to-context — that is, how we behave in any situation — in order to secure our aims, wants, desires, goals, and ambitions.

An^{Y}12

HOPs

General paradigms

Specific paradigms

Meta-paradigm

OUTWARD
ONTOLOGICAL
MANIFESTATIONS

IMPRINTS

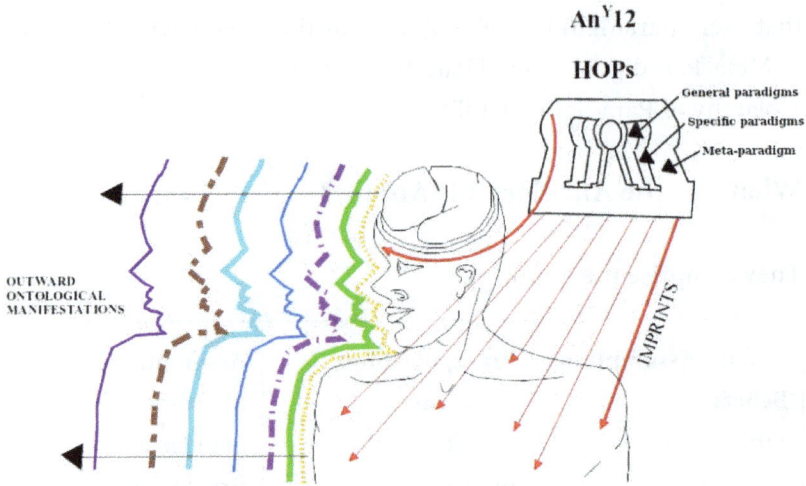

The colours in the above diagram represent our ontologies of being yellow (anxious), feeling blue (sad), being red (with anger), and so forth. Each colour represents a different state of emotion. From this diagram, one can see that

**Our way of Being unfurls from how our
HOPs and An^{Y}14 operate**.

Human ontology can be semantically well formed or ill formed, logically logical or illogically logical, sane or insane, sentient or mad. Whichever it may be, its source, or fountainhead, will lie somewhere in the person's Orthodoxy. Being logical is about following a sequence of thinking in which every step smoothly follows from one to the next. Put simply, thinking is logical when the syntax of Language Structures is smooth in the evolution of its semantics.

A person can be either logical or illogical depending on the situation. Whatever form and manner their thinking takes, there is a logic to a person's logicality and a logic to their illogicality. Put simply, one can have a syntax that is logical or a syntax that is illogical. Put even more simply, one can be logically logical, logically illogical, illogically logical, or illogically illogical.

What we now know is that, in the first instance, one is sane; and in the last, one is insane. For the middle two, we have the jester and the person "talking out of their hat," respectively. Put another way, we will see the grammar of a way of thinking, speaking, feeling, and doing that the average person would conclude is unusual. If a woman insists that she is the Virgin Mary, we can expect her to speak and behave in a way that is illogically illogical. Given that "average" people are in the majority, their response to her is what will count in the end. If she did become extreme in her illogical illogic, she would be incarcerated in a psychiatric unit.

The task of any therapist is to locate where the source is and then to find the Therapeutic Algorithm to unravel it. In doing this, the therapist will cure the person of their problem. Put simply, the critical problem before any therapist is to find out in which sub-system of a paradigm or in which An^{Y}14 the glitch lies.

What we have discovered is you can only find this out if you have the know-how to ask *good questions* — not the *right* question or the *wrong* one, as these take you into the world of Cause and Effect, A, and keep you within the Blame Frame. The *good question* is the question that gets the correct answer by peeling open a problem state and revealing its true nature. For further details, refer to Appendix V: Asking Questions.

Chapter III

The Gifts of Socrates

Socrates gave us two critical gifts. They are as follows:
1. how to ask GOOD QUESTIONS
2. how to recognise what an opinion is

How to Ask GOOD QUESTIONS

From the time I (Dennis) left school, like every other good soul, I had the default assumption that when I asked a question, it was, without a doubt, the right question. However, this changed when I entered Leeds University medical school in 1957 and, for the first time in my life, interacted with undergraduates who were English grammar schoolboys.

Here I was, a graduate of a Jesuit English private school.[4] I was shocked to discover my obvious inadequacies and immaturity relative to my grammar school classmates. It was by overhearing their discussions and praise of Plato's *Symposium* that I learned about Plato. Such was the Jesuitical Roman Catholic bias of my education that I knew about St. Augustine and St. Thomas Aquinas but not Plato or Aristotle.

---

[4] For the benefit of North American readers, a reminder: In Britain, public schools are more exclusive and private schools are less so — the opposite of the North American model.

In time, I did take part in philosophical debates. Looking back, while I thought I fared well in upholding Aquinian philosophical positions, I know that they were being courteous and just putting up with me.

It was then that I bought the *Six Great Dialogues* of Plato. It remained in my collection from 1958 to the present. I remember that, sometime in 1959, I decided to read it. In doing so, especially as I came to the *Symposium*, I felt *as if* I was sitting at the foot of my master, my sensei. I was learning from him that I did not know how to ask *good questions*.

In the *Symposium* I found case after case of critical and crucial debates on high matters of philosophy, politics, education, the military, science, morality, and ethics. Finally, Socrates would enter the debates by just simply asking his questions. And, as he did so, the unrelenting fulcrum of the problem would unravel and the debating issue as a problem was resolved.

When people have problem states, which Richard Bandler described as Stuck States (SS), there is a horrendous debate within them. On the one hand, their intelligence tells them to stop their alcoholism, smoking, gambling, spousal abuse, or overeating, and yet, on the other hand, they keep doing it. This is a conflict that, amazingly, for the great majority of people in Stuck States, their brain power cannot even do a tittle to stop. This must mean that brain power has *no power* to overcome Stuck States. Yet, the obvious revealed ignorance and stupidity of high scholarship keeps insisting on the virtues of mind power, or brain power. The evidence as it stands on the ground does not support it. Will they stop talking rubbish? Guess?

It was my conclusion that there was no one in the University of Leeds or anywhere in the world who could teach me the Art and Science of Asking Socratic Questions. This was to be my fate from 1958 to June 2018.

In 2018, I was toying with the idea of retiring. It began to take its final form, and I decided I would do so in December 2018. By a fortuitous set of circumstances, it turned out to be December 18, 2018. As it turned out, between the beginning of June and December 18, I had fifty new patients.

With my mastery of the languages of A, IL, Ã, 3M, and ~YM — but more critically their respective Virtual Philosophy (VP) and Virtual Logic (VL) — I took it upon myself to see if I could just ask questions about the Stuck States of these patients. To my amazement, I found that just by asking my questions, I was able to resolve their problems.

We then decided to write a book of case examples that validate the effectiveness and efficacy of my Socratic Questions.

Theoretically, five case examples would be sufficient, based on Richard Bandler's Rule of Five, which goes as follows:

1. Solve the first case just by questions, and it is an event.
2. Do it a second time, it is a coincidence.
3. Do it a third time, it's just good luck.
4. Do it a fourth time, the auguries are in your favour.
5. Do it a fifth time — then you are a master at asking *good questions*.

This work was an opportunity to honour George A. Miller. It was he who discovered the law of physics that applied to our minds: that we can retain only seven-plus-or-minus-two chunks of information at any one time at the front of our minds. At a maximum, we can retain only nine chunks. It is for this reason that we decided we would cite nine case examples in our book. Of course, we have entitled our forthcoming work

Just Like Socrates.

In this era of political correctness (PC), opinions are too often treated as facts. However, in our reread of the *Six Great Dialogues*, we discovered that Socrates had a different take on the nature of opinions.

How to Recognise What Opinions Are

Socrates's premise was that there are indeed *facts* in life. He identified positive facts, such as love, kindness, and generosity; and negative facts, such as hate, cruelty, and selfishness. Facts are real.

Then, Socrates asked: What exists in the space between positive and negative facts?

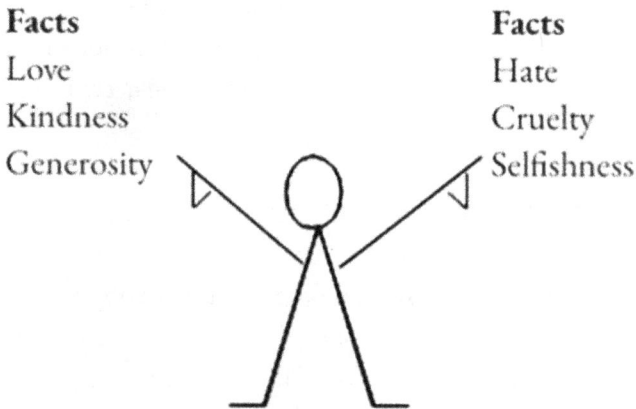

Facts   **Facts**
Love   Hate
Kindness   Cruelty
Generosity   Selfishness

Do you know? We mean no offence, but based on our research, very few people do know. His answer is this:

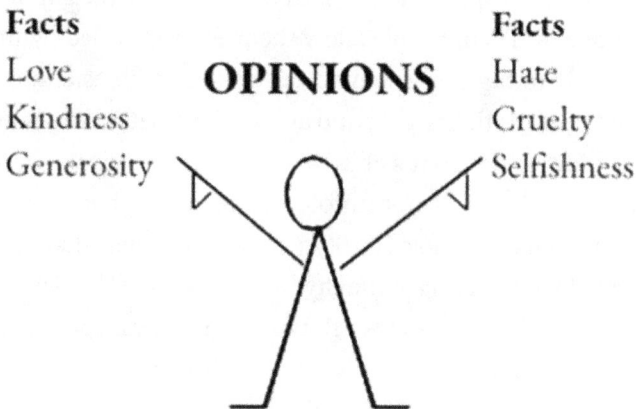

Facts   **OPINIONS**   **Facts**
Love   Hate
Kindness   Cruelty
Generosity   Selfishness

According to Socrates, the space between positive and negative facts is occupied by opinions. In making this point, he clearly distinguishes between facts and opinions in a way that is, sadly, foreign to many people today.

In this day and age, when political correctness reigns supreme and social media platforms are glutted with people swapping opinions, many people treat opinions as fact. This, of course, is nonsensical; unfortunately, in a General Paradigm of A, such opinions seem common sense. For instance, when one says, "You have offended me," the assertion is an opinion. It is not a fact.

Hard as it may be, we all need to grow up and accept the Socratic fact that

OPINIONS ARE NOT — AND CAN NEVER BE — FACTS.

We will explore the above example: "You have offended me." It is implicit in the statement that one person has made or caused the other person to feel offence. But, if we accept the logic of this assertion, then it follows that one can also cause and make another person feel wanton lust (or any other emotion) for someone.

We must all go on our knees and thank the Great Cosmic Mind that no human being has the literal power to *cause* emotions in others or to *make* another feel any emotion whatsoever.

Of course, there are those rare speakers who have the gift of the gab to rah-rah others. Then, people allow themselves to be led by the nose. Hitler had only to tug on his tentacular oratorical fibres and everyone would stand up, raise their right hand and straighten it at the elbow, wrist, and finger joints, and then tug at their vocal cords to yell out "*Sieg Heil!*"

Thankfully, there has not unfolded a person either in Austria or Germany who could assemble 100,000 people in a football stadium and do a repeat performance of a jig to the rhythm of a band of Scottish bagpipes.

However, in the US, a slew of Reborn Evangelical apostles of Jesus Christ seem to be able to do something similar. Of course, unlike Nazism, their gig is to get a **Hallelujah!**

Chapter IV

Modus Ponens

We have already mentioned and briefly defined the modus ponens, which comes to us from the field of Formal Logic. Here, we wish to explore the concept in more detail. As mentioned, in the vernacular, a modus ponens is given by this form of languaging:

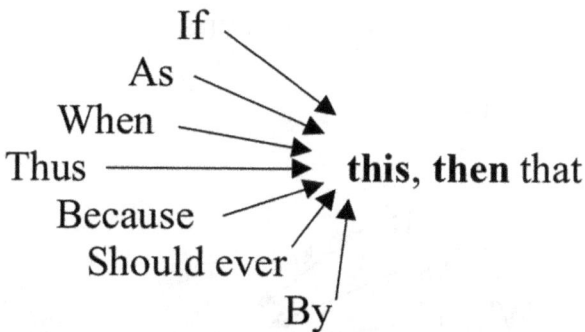

$$
\left.\begin{array}{r}
\text{If} \\
\text{As} \\
\text{When} \\
\text{Thus} \\
\text{Because} \\
\text{Should ever} \\
\text{By}
\end{array}\right\} \text{ \textbf{this}, \textbf{then} that}
$$

As it is so automatic, you are not consciously aware that you are using modus ponens daily in your life. Thus,

If you were nicer to her, **then** she would be nicer to you.
As you continue to miss classes and not hand in your homework, **then** you will end up with a D.
When you get down to visiting your mother more frequently, **then** she will be happier.

Because you resist paying child support, **then** you will be hauled back to court as required.

Should ever you smile and be sweet and gracious, **then** you will discover what a really lovely person she can be.

By your increased effort, **then** you will succeed.

Very few people realise that a modus ponens underpins the study of mathematics. We will take just one example. Consider this equation:

$$C = 2\pi r$$

What do you think this equation is saying?

PAUSE!
GO BACK TO THE EQUATION.
LOOK AT IT AND STUDY IT!
WHAT IS IT SAYING?

Remember this:

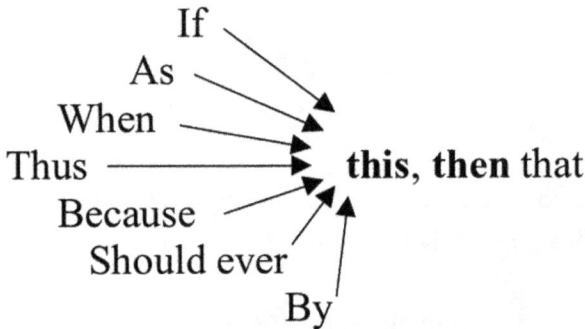

If
As
When
Thus ──────► **this, then** that
Because
Should ever
By

What the equation is saying is

If C has
As C has
When C has
Thus C has ⟶ **this** value **then** r's value is that by 2π
Because C has
Should ever C have
By C having

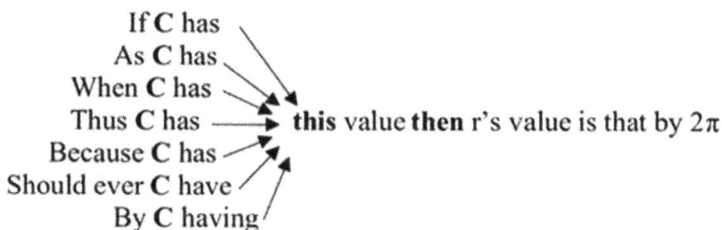

This is how we think and speak; and by the witness of the self-existential experience, thinking mathematically is a natural process in all of us, including children. This raises horrendous and humongous questions, like the following:

1. How is it that we end up with children declaring that they hate math?
2. How is it that our children fail to rank in the top five percent in the international rating of excellence in mathematics?

Respectfully, we must ask: Are our children born with a poor language of maths? Or can it be that our math teachers are incompetent?

The relationship between x and y was once and still is deemed to be causal! Given the fact of modus ponens, the relationship between x and y is functional! In mathematics it is expressed this way:

$$y = f(x)$$

In the vernacular of $\tilde{A}$, the equation translates into "y is a function of x." Thus, you can own a home worth one million dollars, as a function of having that amount of money. You can win your spouse's heart, as a function of having the character, charm, and professional background that you have.

In the vernacular of A, we find causal reasons to blame others — abnegating our responsibility for our actions, thoughts, and feelings. Such vernacular is not based upon the mathematical and logical concept of a modus ponens. By the nature of A, we confine ourselves to the Blame Frame and its consequences.

Chapter V

WHY?

From the day we were born, we were taught to use the interrogative WHY. It was to receive its *imprimatur* when the conjoint father of Western philosophy, Aristotle, declared:

We do not have knowledge of a thing until we have grasped its why, that is to say, its cause!

Since Aristotle said this about WHY, Western civilisation has embraced the question, absolutely and completely.

The first of its consequences is that everyone on Earth uses it without restraint.

The second is that all academic research in all disciplines in every university in the world is spurred and spearheaded by the question WHY.

There are people who think they can use WHY for other purposes. If this is so, they need to be sure that *the intended* information they are seeking by WHY is not about person, method, place, time, choices, specific identity, and specific identity from a set.

What we need to know then, is, what is its linguistic function? We can begin to discover the answer to this question if we break down the functions of all the questions that can be asked.

Question	Linguistic function to get
HOW?	Specific info re: how to do X
WHO?	Specific info re: a person
WHAT?	Specific info re: a thing
WHERE?	Specific info re: a place
WHEN?	Specific info re: a time
WHICH?	Specific info re: a choice
WHOSE?	Specific info re: an identity
WHOM?	Specific info re: an identity from a set of persons
WHY?	Specific info re: evidence relating to guilt or innocence

Go to any judge, prosecuting counsel, defence counsel, barrister, and solicitor and they will confirm to you that the premier question in a court of law, in the end, is WHY. A court needs to have the hard evidence. This might include blood type, fingerprints, DNA, plus the relevant information from the other questions cited in the table above. However, the most important and significant of all questions is WHY! The question seeks the plaintiff's justification for their alleged criminal action. What they say is the critical information that either the judge or the jury has to use in conjunction with the hard evidence to weigh their innocence or guilt.

Put simply, the natural linguistic function of WHY is to get *justification*. If you want information regarding person, place, time identity, and so forth, you have the interrogatives to use. But if you want information regarding guilt or innocence, right or wrong, good or evil, one has to use WHY.

WHY is not the question to ask if you want to get knowledge. Unconsciously, we know that it is for getting *justification*. No human being has the right to ask WHY of another to justify himself. But children are taught to ask WHY — and in doing so with fierce dedication, they can drive their parents homicidal. However, parents do not check their children when they ask WHY? How can they, when they believe it is the way to knowledge?

Unconsciously, people know that when the question is put to them, they are being interrogated as to their motives. They also instinctively know that the fitting answer is *Mind your own business!* However, they know they cannot tell the truth in this age of political correctness. So people lie.

Let us put this to the test. Let's say I were to ask you,

Why do you pick your nose?

The first emotion that peeps up is a touch of offence and anger and the flash of the thought *Who the hell do think you are to dare ask me this question?* The flash is gone and then the real answer wells up:

Mind your own business!

And instantly, PC will not allow you to speak the truth. So, now, whatever your answer might be, it is not the truth. It is a lie.

As for the entire body of research findings in all Western universities, they must now fall into the category of *justification*! Any justification will fall into the category of an opinion. This is validated from the trial judgements when the judge invariably states:

It is therefore <u>the opinion</u> of this court that
you are found guilty of first-degree murder.

In days past, the punishment would be death — and in some places the punishment still is. We had one patient who came to us for a minor problem that we resolved. A few years later, we read in the newspaper that he was convicted of stabbing his wife six times, causing her death. He served only six years in prison and was then released. Such motives exist only in the Blame Frame.

So, the entire body of research in Western universities are *justifications*, which is to say, *opinions*. As such, they are not of the material that are *facts*.

The only discipline that escaped this mess is science. It escaped it because

1. it used the language of mathematics, the modus ponens; and
2. every discovery from the research had to be laboratory tested.

All opinions, regardless of how astute and insightful they might be, were rejected in accordance with the Socratic axiom that opinions are *not* facts.

Chapter VI

The Metalanguage of the Modified Meta Model

We read the musings of philosopher Bertrand Russell about the value and importance of a metalanguage. However, it was such an erudite subject that we were left uninformed as to what precisely is a metalanguage?

The answer slowly unfolded for us. Consider this situation in which these two people are talking with each other, and you are a silent third party listening to them.

blah, blah, blah

yuk, yuk, yuk

A   B

Yes, they are speaking in English — or any language for that matter. At the turn of the century, the field of philosophy began to realise that to understand what they are saying, you have to have a metalanguage. At that time, the notion of a metalanguage did not exist!

It was the conclusion of philosophy and, subsequently, of linguists that to understand what they are saying, you have to have a

LANGUAGE about LANGUAGE!

A language about language is a *metalanguage*.

The value and importance of such a linguistic instrument is explored in the book *Change: Principles of Problem Formation and Problem Resolution* by Paul Watzlawick, John Weakland, and Richard Fisch. In the context of the hierarchical structure of all languages, communication, and learning, the authors point out that to express or explain something "requires a shift to one logical level above what is to be expressed or explained" (79). This is because

> no explaining can be accomplished on the same level; a metalanguage has to be used, but this metalanguage is not necessarily available. To effect change is one thing; to communicate *about* this change is something else: above all, a problem of correct logical typing and of creating an adequate metalanguage. In psychotherapeutic research, it is very common to find that particularly gifted and intuitive therapists think they know why they are doing what they are doing, but their explanations simply do not hold water (79).

As R.D. Laing would write: "If I don't know I don't know, I think I know; if I don't know I know, I think I don't know" (*Knots*, 1972, 55). It is one of these exquisitely fortuitous life events in which the above quote, written in 1974, acknowledges and confirms that "this metalanguage is not necessarily available." One year later, Richard Bandler and John Grinder published *The Structure of Magic: A Book*

About Language and Therapy. In it was the first explicit metalanguage, which the authors called a Meta Model. We had the book, studied it, sat the certification examination by Bandler and Grinder, and passed it.

The Meta Model (2M) was, linguistically, the most powerful information-gathering tool we had encountered. It proved itself as a Therapeutic Algorithm by allowing us to use its language formats to solve problem states. It was Richard Bandler who perceptively realised that all problem states are, in fact, Stuck States. Thus, what is an alcoholic but one who is in a Stuck State? The same can be said of a chronic smoker, cocaine addict, marijuana user, road rager, wife abuser, and so forth. All are stuck in a loop of doing things that do not serve them.

In 1992, we realised that the 2M had been developed within the Blame Frame of the Aristotelian System of Cause and Effect. It was essential to extract the 2M out of the Blame Frame and put it in the Freedom Frame of the Non-Aristotelian System of Relativity and Relatedness. The 2M was too important, therapeutically, to be allowed to remain within the Blame Frame, and we believed the benefits of this Therapeutic Algorithm could be expanded by being reframed within the Freedom Frame. Even the creators of the 2M were trapped within the Blame Frame with its subsequent consequences.

To modify the 2M, linguistic formats had to be critically altered through augmentation. The cause-effect or Blame Frame language of A was taken out of the frame and what was left to replace it was the mathematical language of relativity of $\tilde{A}$. What we ended up with instinctively led us to name our metalanguage the Gathering Information Module (GIM), but in doing so, it seemed we were being disrespectful to Bandler and Grinder. Therefore, we decided to name it the Modified Meta Model (3M), which gave to these two respective discoverers a *logical continuity*.

We teach the 3M in the Power Seminars I and II, which are now in development to transfer online. The seminars were historically taught in Oakville, Ontario. However, if you just want this information, you will find it in our 1993 book, *Power and Elegance in Communication: People, Paradigms and Paradoxes.*

This is one of the more interesting things that we discovered: Each language has its philosophy, and this is, by nature, a Virtual Philosophy. However, once you know a new language, it will carry the logic intrinsic to it and place it into the Virtual Philosophy of the language in you.

When we learned the Meta Model, we could feel a change in our attitude and perspective toward ourselves, others, and the world we live in. However, apart from what we cited here, we cannot tell you specifically what those changes entailed. It is like drinking a superb Chateaux Latour or eating a dish you've never had before and finding it utterly wonderful. If you are asked to explain, specifically, how it was so good, you would be severely tasked to tell it. The French have a saying for this problem: *Je ne sais quoi.* Ultimately, it relates back to people's *opinions.*

By the time we (Dennis and Jennifer) mastered the language of our own creation, the Modified Meta Model, the change in our thinking was even greater. We had completed our transformation from A to $\tilde{A}$, and we were enjoying all the power and elegance that came as a result; we felt that there was no life situation in which we would not feel confident. When one masters the LS of $\tilde{A}$, one finds effortlessness in communication; communication becomes exponentially easier as a means to gather information and resolve issues beyond the confines that depend on blame.

Chapter VII

No-Y-ian Model of Language

The Freedom Seminar teaches the language of Cause and Effect and how we are situated in the Blame Frame of A. The Power Seminars, I and II, teach the alternative: the language of $\tilde{A}$ situated in the Freedom Frame. The No-Y-ian (~YML) Seminar teaches the difference between Meta-Paradigm A and $\tilde{A}$ as we communicate with one another; the individual is taught to move from 2M to 3M. The ~YML is the LS of Relativity from the Freedom Frame.

What is it about? It is about *how to ask the question* that will get you the information about the Intention, Goal, Aim, Purpose, and Desired Outcomes of the other.

In social interactions today, it is generally frowned upon to ask another person too directly about their intentions, goals, aims, purposes, and desired outcomes. We suspect that, especially in this age of PC, it might be deemed intrusive and therefore rude to ask such questions. Yet, from the flow of the text of this work, such questions can have great importance and significance when framed within the language of ~YML. Using the Meta-Paradigm of $\tilde{A}$, we consciously switch our intention from intrusive justification to non-intrusive information.

It is not only about knowing where the person is coming from but where he or she really wants to get to. You can get where a person is coming from and where he or she is at by using the metalanguage of the 3M. However, to understand where someone wants to get to or what they want to get at, you need the ~YML.

Thankfully and mercifully, the ~YML will show you how to ask the questions without giving offence.

For certain aspects relating to asking questions, you will get helpful and worthwhile information from our forthcoming book *Just Like Socrates*. It is the GOOD QUESTION that will peel open for you the true nature of a problem. For further information, see Appendix V.

Chapter VIII

Body Language

By Darwin's theory of evolution, our line of evolutionary descent is from primates. We may surmise that these prehistoric ancestors once lived and thrived in the great canopy of the forests and jungles of the world. In the end, they had to descend to the ground because they evolved to be bipedal. Once they enjoyed the abundance of a wonderful vegan diet. Now on the ground, they were reduced to hunter-gatherers and became prey to the top predators of their day.

They had only their Body Language to communicate with each other. Their Body Language was in their DNA, and when we are born, it is within us. Therefore, we have in us the ability to read Body Language as part of normal communication.

However, Spoken Language (Ad^e) has a far greater efficiency, practicality, speed, proficiency, and utility with respect to the information it can carry.[5] It is for this that we use Spoken Language and sequester BL to one side. But we do so at our own expense. By assigning BL a minor or inferior status relative to Ad^e, we do ourselves a great disservice. Our work and that of FBI agent Joe Navarro, has shown the importance of mastering BL and learning to read it well.

---

[5] **Ad^e** is the cipher created by NLP for the spoken word. Each word is an **Auditory** sound; each word is a digit of language, and it is **externalised** so that a person hears what is uttered. If we are mentally talking to ourselves inside our head, then the code is Ad^i.

To read whether BL is normal or abnormal — insofar as *congruence* between Ad^e (what we say) and BL (what our body does) is concerned (e.g., articulating that you help the poor while walking by someone in need without stopping to help) — we need to have strong abilities in multiple areas. These include the following:

Calibration

All our information is in our Sensory Database (SDB). The SDB comprises these components:

< **Vision Audition Kinaesthesia Olfaction Gustation** >

It is usual to abbreviate the above to only

< V A K O >

These four represent the primary sensory systems and are called the 4-Tuple. In each are their respective linguistic predicates. These linguistic predicates carry their full and rich body of information and knowledge. For example, it is very important in surgery to *look* [V] where you are cutting; if you do not *listen* [A], you will miss what the person is saying; I am in *full empathy* [K] as to how you *feel* [K] about our leadership; he put his plan to us, but it really *smelled* [O] fishy.

When communicating, one has to access the information and items of knowledge, ideas, beliefs, and concepts from one's Sensory Database to say what one wants to say. It was Neuro-Linguistic Programming (NLP) that discovered that a person can detect specific changes in the physicality of another. This, in turn, informs a person regarding which sensory base the other person has gone into to access what they want. Were you to be taught how to refine this ability, think of the advantage you would have in any interaction. You would be described as being ahead of the curve.

For each system we cite five examples. You will have no difficulty thinking of the rest:

Vision (V)	Audition (A)	Kinaesthesia (K)	Olfaction (O)
Look	Hear	Touch	Smell
See	Listen	Feel	Odour
View	Whisper	Smooth	Perfume
Vista	Shout	Rough	Aroma
Outlook	Overhear	Soft	Stench

Calibration involves:

Breathing

If the person's breathing is high in the chest, he is in V (the visual realm) to access the information he wants. When he speaks, he will tell you that he is *seeing* or *looking* to get the visual information. If the person's breathing is in the mid-thorax, he is in A (the auditory realm), getting his information by hearing. If the breathing is abdominal, he is in K, feeling for his information through his bodily, kinaesthetic senses. If one is in olfaction, one is getting information by smell.

Colour of the Cheeks

If the cheeks are pale, the person is in K.
If it is a normal colouring (whatever normal might be for the person in question), he is in A.
If the cheeks are flushed, he is in V.

Hand Movements

If the index finger is pointing, he is in V.
If the palms are flat, he is in A.
If the palms are in a fist, he is in K.

Eye Movements

Eye movements tend to reveal the *most* information about a person's state. The way a person focusses or moves their eyes can let us know which system they are using, as illustrated below.

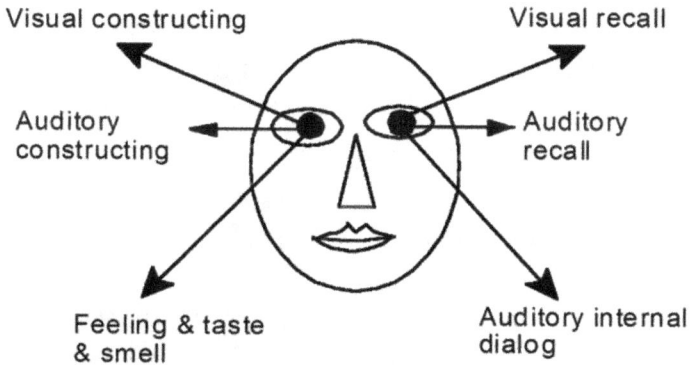

Visual constructing   Visual recall

Auditory constructing   Auditory recall

Feeling & taste & smell   Auditory internal dialog

Pacing and Positioning

The position of the body reveals which of the three accessing cues (i.e., VAK) they are in. If they are slumped over, they are in K. In A, they tend to be pacing backwards to forwards indicating a back and forth of constructing and recalling. In V, they can be in a blaming mode, standing up with finger pointing out.

In our Freedom Seminar workshop on Body Language, we taught participants to gain proficiency and skills in these matters. Currently this workshop is being restructured for an online audience and a forthcoming book.

Adumbration

This is the ability to read the internal state of a person or the state of a given context in life. What is an internal state of a person? It is the emotion that the person is in at that time. It could be anger, frustration, disappointment — or happiness, joviality, or fun. It is only in the context that you will learn to read these states as they are presented to you.

Non-Verbal Communication

If you turn off the sound on the TV, you now see the upper body movements of the anchor person or the entire body of the persons on a discussion panel. What you see is their Non-Verbal Communication. So, what are they communicating to you?

Core Reading of a Person

Speech act theory proposes that, within every utterance, there is a speech act. Consider the following sentences:
- Please come over here.
- I wonder if you might <u>come here</u>.

The speech act of the first sentence is a request, whereas the second sentence is an embedded command (as reflected in the underline). Other speech acts include warnings, invitations, promises, apologies, and predictions. For more information, please refer to Chapter 8 in *Power and Elegance in Communication*. With proper listening, you will notice when people give you clues in their sentences.

We then had to wonder, What would be the equivalent of a speech act in BL? From our research and exploration, we came to these two findings:
1. Every sentence has its speech act, which hinted at a core issue. The speech act is not always congruent with BL (e.g., you may say yes while your body is clearly indicating no).
2. Every act or movement has to stem from one source that, at that moment, was the specific Being of the person. Thus, the core issue of personhood was extant at that moment for that

context. The Core Reading, therefore, required the skill of the other three above (Calibration, Adumbration, Non-Verbal Communication) to read the core personhood accurately for any given life situation and given the multivalent nature of the An^Y14.

If you can master the skill to do this well, you will be in a singular position of power and control in that life situation.

Chapter IX

Orbital Trajectory of Life

In the vernacular, we speak of Being on our path in life. However, the field of Neuro-Semantic Programming recognises that life is hierarchical and relational. We are all at some level relative to others — either vertically or laterally.

We all achieve our level in life. Put simply, we are now in our orbit. And we arrive at our orbit by the power of the Virtual Philosophy (VP) of the two-language system that we have — the Aristotelian world of Cause and Effect (A) and Informal Logic (IL). It is our VPs that are the rocket engines that take us to our orbit.

Once upon a time, it was the norm that there was no way for a person to shift their orbit to a higher level. It did sometimes happen after a critically significant life event impacted a person. Their thinking and Being changed. Sometimes it was for the worse, and the person became an alcoholic. Sometimes the person soared to a higher orbit and found ways to new wealth, esteem, and distinction in life.

Now we have discovered these new language systems:

1. the language of the Non-Aristotelian System of Relativity and Relatedness (Ã)
2. the metalanguage of the Modified Meta Model (3M)
3. the No-Y-ian Model of Language (~YML)
4. the Body Language (BL)

Each of these languages has its own Virtual Philosophy. If you master these first three languages, a rocket will ignite in your unconscious and automatically take you out of your current orbit of life to a different and higher orbit. Yes, your life will change, and it will do so seamlessly, in accord with your unconscious decisions and wishes. It will all happen so naturally.

Chapter X

Human Anger

Every human being has the ability to generate a vast array of possible feelings or emotions. We have elected to use Anger because it is an archetypal example for all feelings or emotions.

What few people know is that the emotions of significance and importance in a person are the drivers for them to be the way-they-are-to-context. You already know-how-to-be unconsciously, after all, by way of your Epistemology and your Orthodoxy. For instance, a man may explode with increasing levels of anger within seconds over another's uncommon sense to bring an old carpet found on the side of street to a shared home. The carpet, meant for a woodworking project, could (or could not) contain cockroach eggs and bedbugs, despite assurances that the carpet was thoroughly cleaned.

Human emotions fall into two categories. There are those that belong to the Light Side of the Force and those to the Dark Side. These are the two extremes of Aristotle's facts; what lies between is based upon our opinions. The Light Side of the Force entails love, happiness, bliss, harmony, and so forth, and the Dark Side of the Force sinks us into despair, depression, fear, anxiety, and so forth. We see such polarity in all primordial symbolism (man, woman; day, night; solar, lunar), which we call the Reality of Opposites derived from Joseph Campbell's "power of opposites," detailed in his many works.

We all think. We think by our *minds*; but we also think by our *Being*. By our minds, we think by *thoughts*; and by our Being, we think by *feelings*.

Thoughts and feelings are *about* something, be it animal, vegetable, mineral, or an event. An *about* of anything is by definition an *opinion* about it. Here are two isomorphic examples:

1. I really think that Jimmy is an idiot.
2. I really feel that Jimmy is an idiot.

All feelings have these structural features to them:

*   quality
*   intensity
*   scale

Anger can have a homicidal quality to it; it can be at a very high level of intensity, and its scale can be focussed on one target. For this, it consumes an incredible amount of energy. Normally, such an expenditure of energy cannot be sustained by the physiology of a person. If, by their will, they persist, they will eventually collapse.

One's anger cannot remain at a fever pitch for very long. Eventually, a person has to get back to the business of living. But this raises a problem because the anger doesn't just go away. It remains inside the person and will go on churning and churning.

Is it a good thing to bear anger against another indefinitely? Rationally, it is not. If it is not, then, in the Reality of Opposites between good and evil, it — the act of maintaining anger — is *evil*. And this evil will do everything possible to give to such a person a long life so that the unconscious withering and suffering by the churning of the anger can go on and on. It will not support an end to such a person's life, because that would be a merciful act; and it is just not in the nature of evil to be merciful.

If you are an active participant in your community, you may hear gossip about who in the community is considered to be evil or wicked.

And when you check, you will find that they are invariably living a long life. For out of this comes this truth that

Only the GOOD die young!

In other words, EVIL persists and subsists long after the person passes on. The Yorkshire Ripper comes to mind. If you continue to be angry and simmer on such ill-formed Orthodoxy situated in A, then consequences are inevitable, whether physically, emotionally, or mentally. So let it go!

Chapter XI

Human Violence and War

In his book *On Aggression*, Konrad Lorenz describes our inhumanity to kith and kin through our perennial tilt to *war*. From Day One of our emergence onto the stage of life on Earth, humans have enacted violent attacks against other groups of humans. Violence, of course, occurs throughout the animal kingdom. For example, chimpanzees will attack another troop of chimps to steal their food. But they do not invoke by action the mass killing of another troop of chimpanzees. Humans are the only ones who do such atrocities as war against each fellow humans.

Western civilisation has its roots in ancient Greece. It is recorded in the texts that the polity of Greece was divided into autonomous city-states. Such was their inter-relating that the curse of their warring with each other was taken as a way of life.

In their warring, the victors claimed the spoils, including human survivors. Those survivors became slaves. If the victors captured a city, it was typical to rape and kill its citizens. The survivors were enslaved and all property became the chattel of the conquerors. The city was put to the torch. This happened to Troy when King Agamemnon took it. When Alexander conquered the magnificent ancient capital of Persepolis of the ancient Persian Empire of Darius and Xerxes, he put it to the torch. It was an act of brute vandalism. When Scipio took the city of Carthage and ended Carthaginian civilisation, the city was put to the torch. What do you think Genghis Khan did to the wonderful ancient city of Samarkand?

Our technology and weaponry in the business of doing war has improved exponentially from the later part of the nineteenth century to today. Remember the instant evaporation of the cities of Hiroshima and Nagasaki? Some two hundred thousand people vanished off the face of the earth; and the survivors faced hideous consequences from radiation exposure.

Was the above event a *good* thing to do? If you say it is not, then in the Reality of Opposites, it is *evil*. It is this evil that will see to the extended longevity of a nation that was responsible for what happened. And this evil will wither this nation to its end. Its end will be *astounding*. Did you know that when Rome fell, there was a joyous celebration! However, one aspect of its evil continued. It was their barbaric Games, which lasted for another four hundred years before an edict ended them.

Chapter XII

Therapeutic Algorithms

Psychiatry is a logical system with its Orthodoxy and Virtual Philosophy. As a result, there are very few in medicine who are aware that, if one really wishes to cure a person of mental illness, that is, to bring about Second-Order Change (IIOC), the operator has to apply a Therapeutic Algorithm (TA). This idea was first proposed by Richard Bandler and John Grinder (B&G) for their cure of aerophobia. They invented their TA, which they named the Flying Phobia Cure. It was an amazing and most timely discovery.

It was amazing because, in approximately one hour, the person was cured of their fear of flying. It was a most timely discovery because it happened when the airline industry introduced chartered flights. This resulted in affordable airfares for many people in the West and a significant number of people in the rest of the world. Just as flights became more affordable, thousands of people discovered that they had a fear of flying. The offices of professionals in the field of caring for people with mental ill health were inundated with these new clients.

Before Bandler and Grinder developed their TA, there was no cure for aerophobia. I came up with the best I could think of at the time. It was for the flyer to take 5 mg of Valium and a double shot of vodka. This was the Chong V&V treatment for aerophobia. The person who wanted to fly was to take the treatment as soon as possible after getting on the plane. It would ideally sedate the person and hopefully overlap (i.e., guide) them into sleep for a three-hour flight from Toronto to Miami, Florida, for example. If the person had to fly longer, they would have to repeat the V&V drug schedule as required for longer flights.

Psychiatry came up with a method to cure aerophobia that they named desensitization. It was a costly and time-consuming regime, and it was to prove relatively unsuccessful. However, not all mental illnesses need to be cured by a pill (or can be).

Such was the effectiveness and efficacy of B&G's Therapeutic Algorithm of Flying Phobia Cure that the diagnostic was for all purposes eliminated. Since then, the one-hour Flying Phobia Cure has been reduced to six minutes. For this, it is now known as Bandler and Grinder's Six-Minute Flying Phobia Cure. Since then, our research has taken us in the following directions:

1. Determining what was the Ontological Equation ($On^T Eq^N$) or the Ontological Theorem ($On^T Th^M$) of a given mental illness; such an equation or theorem maps the processes of our Orthodoxy within the VAKOG system for a given thought or behaviour. An example would be a near-simultaneous $V^c V^r K^e$ to represent the visual construct of stress, the visual recall of the memory stress, and then the kinaesthetic behaviour of biting nails.

2. Determining what was the Therapeutic Algorithm (TA) that would unravel the given $On^T Eq^N$ or $On^T Th^M$ and, in doing so, cure the person.

What few people appreciate in the idea of the Reality of Opposites is the implication that

Every normal thinking has its natural opposite.

Or put another way (using our own terminology),

Every normal $On^T Eq^N$ has its natural abnormal variant.

This means that the possibility of abnormal thinking could stretch into infinity. Therefore the 700+ diagnostics that appear in the book *Diagnostic and Statistical Manual of Mental Disorders*, Fifth Edition, (*DSM-5*) could stretch into the trillions! It is for this that our explorations and findings into TAs are only just beginning. We will share them with you so you will also recognise their existence as an alternative.

Naturally, these TAs are to be learned through the care and patience of a qualified practitioner. Mastering these TAs lies beyond the scope of our book, or any book for that matter. The TAs do exist, and we now place before you what we currently have. Each one has its own application for the specific Stuck State; for some states, multiple TAs are required. Those labelled † are from B&G.

TA† for Aerophobia
Search the internet and you will be astounded by the number of possible phobias. It has been found by graduate students of NLP and NSP that the B&G TA for aerophobia can be used to cure other phobias, from achluophobia (fear of darkness) to zoophobia (fear of animals).

TA† for Change History
We learned from Milton Erickson to guide a person into an existential experience whose properties are such that it will extract them out of the system of logic that they are stuck in to another, better system of logic. The manoeuvre of Change History from B&G does exactly this. The result is that you can free a person of their crippling false belief and of the negative imprints of their life trauma.

TA of Analog Contracts
We discovered the structure of this TA from a paper that Milton Erickson wrote about how he cured a couple with nocturnal enuresis. You will find this article in his book *Advanced Techniques of Hypnosis and Therapy*, edited by Jay Haley (pp. 410–412). In this TA, it is essential that you contract with the client that they will do the

prescribed treatment. Only after they agree to the verbal contract —
cemented in a shaking of hands — do you *then* prescribe the
treatment. The importance of a contract is the creation of an
agreement between two people that gets them to recognise what they
are doing.

There is a diagnosis in psychiatry known as trichotillomania. Put
simply, it is persistent hair pulling. In psychiatry, we have read that
this problem is designated as incurable. Epiepistemologically, of
course, it is curable because we have the TA for it.

TAs for the Emotions of the Dark Side of the Force

There are a huge scan of Emotions of the Dark Side that unfold in us.
Here we deal with only a few, including disappointment, anger,
frustration, bitterness, sadness, and depression.

What few people realise is that these and other Dark-Side
emotions are inevitable components of the Language Structure (LS)
that dwells in us. What is this Language Structure? It is *should* or
should not. As an LS, your *should* has a vast number of personal
expectations. These expectations are not reasonable, natural, or
legitimate; instead, they carry a misplaced sense of entitlement.

Is it not true that every time that you have an *expectation* that fails
you, you instantly feel some combination of disappointment, anger,
frustration, bitterness, sadness, and depression? All too soon, you are
looking for someone or something to blame for these feelings. But the
feelings stem from the misplaced expectation.

Now let us put this to you: Do we not live in a reality of the
unknown in which *there are no guarantees, sureties, and certainties*?
In such a reality,

Are you sane or insane to have *expectations*?

What is the TA to be free of *shoulds/should nots* and *expectations*
and the Dark Side? The TA for the aforementioned is by guiding the
individual out of the Blame Frame and into the Freedom Frame.

TA† of Compelling Referential Experience (CRE)

B&G found that there are life experiences that critically imprint on our BL. As a result, there are certain unhelpful learnings that we are forever referring to so that we reuse them in our life. B&G created the CRE to clean this.

A critical example of such a negative life experience is parents consistently telling their developing, evolving child that they are no good and will never amount to anything. An even worse example is sexual abuse.

TA for Healing the Wound of Sexual Abuse

In the case of sexual abuse, you undo the negative impacts of the mechanical aspects of the abuse through CRE. When it is done, what you are left with is the wound of emotions. You have to apply a TA for its healing.

In our conjoint practice, we agreed that Jennifer would be the person to deal with all sexual abuse cases that came to us. As Jennifer became better and better in her skills in this area, we knew there was still more to know about how to heal the sex abuse wound. Where were these words of healing? As it turned out, we could not find them in the Torah, the New Testament, the Quran, the Analects of Confucius, the Mayan Popol Vuh, the Vedas, or the samples of Buddhist scriptures that came into our hands. Then, one day, in my hands was the book written by the first Jain priest who left India to come to North America. As I read it, I became more and more sure that here were healing words. I selected four parts of it and typed them out. Thus, I handed to Jennifer the copies of the teachings of Gurudev I, II, III, and IV of inner healing through guided imagery in a hypnotic state. GI had an incredible value to uplift a person, while GII was excellent for healing verbal and physical trauma. GIII was the healer of the sex abuse wound, and GIV was best for specific traumas. As always, a direct experience is better than simply reading; moreover, these teachings aren't uniformly applied; the imagery and words used are particular to the space, place, and time of the An^{Y}14.

TA of Identification Therapy

This TA was discovered by us in the fall of 2019. Our identification oddly finds its ultimate encapsulation in our passport. I (Dennis) am a Canadian citizen, a Canadian husband, a Canadian father, a Canadian host, a Canadian taxpayer, and so forth. However, if my wife wants to, we can up sticks and immigrate back to England, and then we can change our identity and recover the Englishness that we lost.

One of my adult patients had been physically beaten to an inch of his life when he was younger. It created an Ontological Theorem (On^TTh^M) that spun a cluster of symptoms out of him, for which, over the years, as each unfolded, I had to find a TA to undo. This work led to a very good friendship between us. I had every intention of sustaining our friendship, but there was a part of me that deeply wanted to reach the end between us with him as a client and me as his clinician.

So, upon his return after his usual two to three months away and after our fond civilities for each other, he then blurted out to me:

I now know I have found my real problem.
I hate my father!

When I heard this, my heart leapt with joy. This was it. With the TA from Identification Therapy, we finally arrived at the closure of our link as client and clinician. Identification Therapy brings a patient back to the CRE so that the healing of the CRE occurs. Then there is an emotional tear or wound that needs to be closed. Serious emotional tears require stitching so that the wound can be closed completely and left in the past. We are speaking symbolically for when patients are in a trance state — the wound or tear is very real, if intangible.

I did the TA and, upon conclusion, he verified he felt tremendous peace and calm. We have kept in touch since.

TA to Reverse a Cancer

There are two distinct Ontological Equations attached to a cancer:

1. the On^TEq^N that produces the cancer
2. the On^TEq^N that regenerates the cancer

These two On^TEq^Ns are very different. In many cases, medicine cures the actual cancer. There is not a trace of it anywhere, but the On^TEq^N that has the power to regenerate it is there — intact in the person. It is only *waiting for the occasion* to know it is time to regenerate the cancer. If the occasion never exists again, the patient will be cancer-free until it is time for them to join *the light*. If the occasion is there for it to reactivate itself, it will do so. If the occasion is a ferocious exacerbation, the reactivated cancer will be ferociously malignant. Thus, within three weeks of the return of his leukaemia, my friend died. My task was to deliver the eulogy at his funeral.

The TA for the inversion of a cancer is done via the Universal Induction Protocol that Jennifer and I discovered.

You are required to find the On^TEq^N for which there is a specific TA that will undo it. In the latest case we were working with, it was

> I cannot go on living with a man
> who so utterly disrespects me!

Of course, once I found it, I asked my patient to close her eyes and to listen to me as I said the above line and to nod if it was indeed true to her Being. She listened to it. Then, slowly and deliberately, she nodded.

As an On^TEq^N, it took about an hour to undo the logic of it.

To work out, any On^TEq^N requires you to have mastery over these language systems. The process is as follows:

with **unconscious** facility & cognitive **unawareness** to **conscious** facility & cognitive **awareness**	the language of the Aristotelian System of Cause and Effect (A) and the language formats of Informal Logic (IL)
with **conscious** facility & cognitive **awareness** to **unconscious** facility & cognitive **unawareness**	the language of the Non-Aristotelian System of Relativity and Relatedness (Ã) the metalanguage of the Modified Meta Model (3M) and the No-Y-ian Model of Language (~YML), which incorporates the following: 1. Body Language 2. Calibration 3. Adumbration 4. Core Read of the persona at that moment in time

TA[†] of the Reframe

When there is a Stuck State that needs understanding from a different point of view, then we rely on the Reframe TA from B&G. It is very simple to do this TA. It requires only alertness, awareness, and wit. You go meta to what the person is saying and determine what intellectual/mental frame they are operating out of. Once you know that, your next task is to find the best alternative frame to guide them into, to reframe the situation. The reframing allows help from other parts of the person's body to change their behaviour or way of thinking. For example, we found success with infertility through the application of reframing by addressing the uterus.

TA[†] of Inverting a Person's Life Criterion, Standard, and Metric

If you know a person's most highly valued criterion, standard, and metric for suborning others, all you need to do is wait for the opportunity to use it on them. For example, take a person who is dead set against abortion. We can then ask: What is meaningful about having an abortion? Thereafter, we can relay a true story of a thirteen-year-old girl whose father is also her grandfather. Moreover, the numerous associated risks that come with such a predicament — genetic and otherwise. In such a way, we invert the life criterion back to the one dead set against abortion. This is just a simple example among many.

TA† of Metacommenting
Put simply, this TA from B&G is about the ability and skill to come up with an opinion or statement that will compel a volte-face in a person. The TA allows the person to understand another point of view, which has life-changing possibilities through acceptance.

TA to Become a Genius
We have discovered the TA to secure a Second-Order Change (IIOC) of a person whose thinking is average into that of a genius. The main idea behind this TA is to help them discover the power within their own Being that can put them on an alternative path to feeling stuck. The first test case that we have is a student who got his BSc in computer science. I then persuaded him to do his MSc in computer science. Finally, I persuaded him to do a PhD in computer science. He has elected get his PhD in AI.

I decided to offer this TA to him. Following this, he sent me a report regarding what has been happening to his mentation. He is becoming more and more aware that he has a better grasp of new AI knowledge.

TA for Ending a State of Chronic Grief
Grieving can be a curse that can last for years and can leave a person crippled and impoverished. Yet by our TA, it can be ended in one working session. The key is to get them to go back to the time just before the person's death and to have them share with the deceased anything that they feel was left unsaid. Thereafter, still in the trance

state, to guide them back to the light for the recently deceased, telling them that you love them or that they are loved.

TA of Therapeutic Metaphors

It was David Gordon who first identified the power of Parables-in-Therapy, as cited in his book, *Therapeutic Metaphor*. As many know, Jesus Christ taught his disciples using parable after parable. Such was its ontological and epistemological power that, after his death, these twelve fishermen stepped onto the world stage and renounced the religion of the Roman Empire for the religion of Christianity. A therapeutic metaphor involves finding what metrics you are to cull. Then you construct the parable/metaphor that carries the contrarian metrics that generates the person's problem state.

TA of Timeline

The theory of Being on a timeline involves being either *future-orientated* or *present-orientated* or *past-orientated*.

Depending upon the direction we use, the outcome can be either positive or negative. For example, the person who is future-orientated tends to be very impatient if they propel themselves too far ahead, so they cannot enjoy the now. The positive side is that they can see opportunities and situations they can work toward.

If you are present-orientated, it is the now that is up front. In the teachings of Mindfulness, this is a good thing. However, a lot depends upon the time frame of a person's now. It can be a minute, a day, a week, a month, or even a year. The positive can be that you live in the moment and enjoy it. The negative is that, if there are many things to do in the present with time limits, you can feel overwhelmed and even be accused of procrastinating.

If you are past-orientated, this means your focus is always on checking the past and usually involves comparing the past and future. The negative side is that the future has not happened yet and, if the past has flashing neon lights of negative events, you can be stuck in memories.

Each of the above timeline orientations has its own way of being, so the TA is to change the direction of the timeline and to check it and address any situations where they may be stuck.

TA of Past Life

A past life situation is very different from a past experience in the present life, although they can be connected. There are some present problem states, such as anxiety or insomnia, which have turned out to be connected to a past life experience. This becomes obvious in the case where, no matter what you do, nothing changes. The person may even say, "It is as if I have had the problem all my life."

The TA is to guide the person inward, in whichever hypnosis trance induction you are familiar with. Go to the time that is the root of the problem and find out what they came to believe that they brought into their present life that needs to be addressed and resolved.

Above, we have listed the TAs that are currently available. As always, with time, we are hoping that new TAs will be discovered to meet the needs of future times.

Chapter XIII

Ill-Formed Human Nature

Our discussion of ill-formed Human Nature (HN) will benefit from a deep dive into one of our fascinations: Chef Robert Irvine and his television series, *Restaurant Impossible*.

In his show, he tries to save restaurants that are at the point of shutting down from lack of business or mismanagement or any number of other problems. We found that all these restaurants have the following in common:

1. The principal owner or co-owners were ill-formed in their respective Human Nature between themselves, toward the kitchen staff, and toward the serving staff.

2. If a principal owner was married, the marriage was at its breaking point because both parties were ill-formed in their HN toward each other.

3. The principal owner or co-owners had an exalted ego, overly bloated self-esteem, and an exaggerated self-importance.

4. The principal owner or co-owners were "always right."

5. The front of the restaurant was often in poor condition — the floor was sticky, the furniture was old, worn, and torn, and in some cases the bar was partially gummed up with material that was a breeding place for salmonella.

6. In certain extreme cases, the condition of the back of restaurant was such that, if officers of the Public Health

Department had come in, they would require the restaurant to shut down at once. Chef Irvine found cockroaches in such kitchens and sometimes dead mice.

7. The respective Human Nature of each staff at the front of the restaurant were such that they were fighting among themselves and, in some cases, they were arrogant and disobedient to senior staff.

It is hard to imagine any psychiatrist coming in and, within forty-eight hours, being able to

- turn the ill-formed Human Nature of such failed restaurant owner or co-owners into being well formed;
- guide a crew to redo the entire restaurant so that it is a new one;
- reverse negative revenue at a rate of $2,000 to $4,000 per month to grossing more than $1,000,000 and paying off a $350,000 debt within four to seven years.

The entire psychiatric profession needs to see the series of *Restaurant Impossible*. In doing so, they would be forced to admit that all their theorizing about the psycho-bio-mechanics of mental ill health must be nonsensical drivel. To illustrate just how pernicious these failures have been within psychiatry, we have included (in Appendix I) the full text of Loren R. Mosher's letter, in which he explains why he is quitting the professional association and critiques the entire field of psychiatry as it was practised then and is practised now — for the benefit of pharmaceutical companies.

Of course, there may be some television magic involved in making this show's victories seem so certain and the transformation of each restaurant and all the restauranteurs and staff more seamless and dramatic than they might have been in reality. Even so, and even if the results are distorted or exaggerated by half, we would still argue that Chef Irvine accomplishes more in a short span of time than virtually any psychiatrist could do under the circumstances. Part of his success may have to do with motivation.

By the time he gets to his latest case, the owners of the restaurants are in desperate need of his help. His clients are in such deep doo-doo that they *have* to accept his guidance. Psychiatrists have to motivate their clients to do things, and we suspect that, in many cases, they fail.

For psychiatry, what we can truly, humbly, and respectfully say, is this:

> Here before you is the witness to Yoda's advice to Luke Skywalker: You have to unlearn what you have learnt.

In his desperate appeal to the president of the American Psychiatric Association, Loren R. Mosher explained the main problem with psychiatry as follows:

> These psychopharmacological limitations on our abilities to be complete physicians also limit our intellectual horizons. No longer do we seek to understand whole persons in their social contexts, rather we are there to realign our patients' neurotransmitters. The problem is that it is very difficult to have a relationship with a neurotransmitter, whatever its configuration.

The paradigm that holds that our ontology is a function of the balance and alignment of our brain chemicals and neurotransmitters fails before the thrones of common sense and intellectual wit. And it is corroborated by the fact that, to date, not one of these multibillion-dollar pharmacological companies have been able to find one chemical that can rebalance the imbalance of the errant brain chemicals and neurotransmitters or realign the misaligned neurotransmitters.

Maybe there is a conflict of interest here. If they did find such a chemical, their revenue from the sale of such a drug for mental illnesses would fall, since it would cure the person of his mental illness. So, they have a built-in disincentive to finding the cure. If this is true, these drug companies are acting *illegally*, *immorally*, and *unethically*.

Conclusion

There were semantic issues of deep concern that inspired us to write this work. There were so many things about these semantic issues in life that challenged the precious traces of our past beliefs and attachments. We suspect that some of the content might do the same for you. However, at the same time, we hope that there are many new learnings and ah-ha moments that you can take with you and use wisely in your everyday life, whether professionally or socially or both.

We began by asking the question, What is a cure when it applies to a mental disorder? In order to answer this question, we first had to map out how E^{epi} related back to our pre-Socratic roots. Once we were made aware that there is an extension beyond Epistemology, we began our research to knowing-how-another-knows-to-be. We paid homage to how HN is a difficult beast to tame in that it self-replicates throughout time through our Orthodoxy. We recognised, early on in our research that there are two Meta-Paradigms, A and Ã, with their subsequent LSs and VPs, through which we come to know the world. We recognised that the A of Cause and Effect implicated the individual in the Blame Frame. Over many works and research, we have advocated for a Freedom Frame of Relativity: Ã.

In our research, we sought to uncover the methods to change one's Orthodoxy from ill-formed states to those which are well-formed. The process entails learning the ~YML. In so doing, we can unblock semantic Stuck States of an individual's ontology. The way to unravel Stuck States is through the 3M and asking GOOD questions. Once you have the answer, you can then reliably attend to these states through the use of a TA with its associated analog contract. As we are dealing with the semantics of the problem — instead of the linguistics — we chose to call our program NSP. NSP uses the Freedom Frame of $\bar{A}$ instead of the Blame Frame of A.

Learning how to operate within the LS of $\bar{A}$ was historically taught through successive Power Seminars I and II and was detailed in our work *Power and Elegance in Communication*. All these ideas and efforts culminated in the development of TAs within $\bar{A}$.

What we are after concerns Human Nature and how we can change it. We now know we live our life based upon our Orthodoxy with its systems within systems and its respective ontology and Epistemology. The LS of Cause and Effect creates ill-formed Human Nature and abnegates personal responsibility.

To change Human Nature, one needs to learn to read BL, ask GOOD questions, and listen to the LS that another is using. Doing so and identifying what needs to be changed is made possible using the seminars, the TAs, and/or hypnosis. In our last chapter, we listed all the TAs available in our practice.

With the completion of this work, there may be more challenges ahead for us. After all, learning never stops. There is always some new research or unanticipated situation or event that can change our lives in an instant. The best we can hope for is to use the tools we have to overcome the everyday challenges with grace and impeccability.

Glossary of Terms

4-Tuple is the term for Vision, Kinaesthetic, Audition, Olfaction.

Adumbration is the means by which we generally sense another in a situation and assess things like whether they are angry or happy.

Analog Contract (AC) refers to a contract in which a person agrees to follow a specific set of TA procedures.

An^{Y}14 stands for a person's ancillary life metrics. They include (1) default assumptions, (2) beliefs, (3) ethics, (4) criteria, (5) customs, (6) presuppositions, (7) opinions, (8) metrics, (9) biases, (10) traditions, (11) assumptions, (12) morality, (13) standards, and (14) prejudices.

Aristotelian System of Cause and Effect (A) is a powerful language system that operates by a logical structure derived from its philosophy called Causality. It is also an all-encompassing life blueprint that determines the operations of all General Paradigms and Specific Paradigms that trap one unconsciously in the Blame Frame.

Blame Frame refers to a specific LS of A that is seen in speech acts (e.g., "You made me do it" or "I feel this way because of you").

Body Language (BL) refers to the physical cues that the body gives. It reveals various states that can be calibrated and adumbrated.

Calibration is the reading of the finer details of a person's *specific* physical features, including breathing, colour of the cheeks, hand movements, eye movements, and pacing and positioning.

Compelling Referential Experience (CRE) refers to an event in the past that is still active emotionally in the present.

Core Reading is our understanding, through reading the person's Body Language, of the person's various paradigms (HOPs) and ancillaries (An^{Y}14), such as their beliefs. Core Reading ultimately demonstrates one's personhood.

Epiepistemology (E^{epi}), also known as Neuro-Semantic Programming, refers to the study of how to ask specific questions and get the answer to the question of how the other knows-to-know-to-be. With the answer, one would be able to understand another — whether in therapeutic or pragmatic applications.

First-Order Change (IOC) refers to a change of a situation within the same frame (e.g., moving the furniture around a room, giving it a new perspective; or a person who stops smoking and then starts to drink).

Function can mean any of the following: the relationship, role, use, value, action, or its work. So, the function of money, lever, soup spoon, or chopsticks is about the role of the item between one person and another, a thing or a situation. Mathematically, *function* is written this way: f(x).

Holarchy of Paradigms (HOPs) refers to the bubble or our map of the world in which we store all the information involving An^{Y}14, our experiences, and our paradigms in a relational and hierarchical way.

Informal Logic (IL) is a theoretical alternative to Formal Logic for use in everyday life and reasoning. A joke would be Informal Logic as it does not follow the logical structure of Formal Logic.

Language Structure (LS) is a file/cabinet/designation/label for a topic of consideration that has/contains/holds all the semantic material and the entire vocabulary from which the owner of the LS sources all ideas, writing, and speaking about the given topic.

Meta Model (2M) is a Gathering Information Module that is structured in the language system of Cause and Effect (A).

Meta-Paradigm refers to A and Ã.

Modified Meta Model (3M) is our revision to the Meta Model (2M) of the NLP tradition into the LS of Relativity and Relatedness (Ã).

Neuro-Linguistic Programming (NLP) is the study of language and the structure of ontology and deals with specific body-reading techniques and reframing situations in A. Co-founded by Richard Bandler and John Grinder (B&G), NLP reveals how we think.

Neuro-Semantic Programming (NSP) is the study of semantics behind the language (i.e., the *meaning* of language) and is our theoretical extension of NLP, which is not embedded in A, and looks at whole body reading in Ā. NSP reveals *who we are*.

Non-Aristotelian System of Relativity and Relatedness (Ā) refers to the Freedom Frame.

No-Y-ian Model of Language (~YML) refers to our clever use of *Don't ask WHY* in a new LS in Ā.

Ontological Equation (On^{T}Eq^N) is the equation that determines the unique way of thinking and Being in a person at any given time and context. It is the sequence of thinking/metamentation.

Ontological Theorem (On^{T}Th^M) is the process of acquiring the Ontological Equation.

Ontology is a field of study that explores the fabric of human subjective reality and, by extension, the foundations of human sentience, or our way of Being. The study of Ontology seeks to discover the critical elements that constitute the structure of human subjective experience.

Paradigm is a blueprint, map, plan, or design. There are three types of paradigms: General Paradigms, Specific Paradigms, and Meta-Paradigms. Our paradigms can be our race, culture, language, and so on. These are holarchically layered to form our HOPs.

Second-Order Change (IIOC) is a change of a situation beyond the same frame (e.g., waking up from multiple nightmares, or pulling the house down and rebuilding).

Semantic Paradigm is a blueprint to get an understanding of a large semantic domain of consideration.

Sensory Database (SDB) refers to the site in the brain where we locate our visual, auditory, kinaesthetic, olfactory, and gustatory information. These letters stand for the different senses of the SDB — V, A, K, O, G.

Therapeutic Algorithms (TAs) are used to heal Stuck States.

Virtual Logic (VL) is the logical structure of the semantic system of VP.

Virtual Philosophy (VP) refers to the associated philosophy of a particular language that resides in the body and is expressed through Body Language.

Appendix I

The Loren R. Mosher Letter

Sent: Thursday, August 26, 1999 6:41 AM
Subject: PSYCHIATRIST DISSOLVES 35-YEAR ASSOCIATION
WITH AMERICAN PSYCHIATRIC ASSOCIATION

Loren R. Mosher, MD

December 4, 1998

To,

Rodrigo Munoz, MD, President
American Psychiatric Association

Dear Rod:

After nearly three decades as a member it is with a mixture of pleasure and disappointment that I submit this letter of resignation from the American Psychiatric Association.

The major reason for this action is my belief that I am actually resigning from the American Psychopharmacological Association. Luckily, the organization's true identity requires no change in the acronym. APA reflects, and reinforces, in word and deed, our drug dependent society. Yet, it helps wage war on "drugs".

"Dual Diagnosis" clients are a major problem for the field but not because of the "good" drugs we prescribe. "Bad" ones are those that are obtained mostly without a prescription.

A Marxist would observe that being a good capitalist organization, APA likes only those drugs from which it can derive a profit — directly or indirectly. This is not a group for me. At this point in history, in my view, psychiatry has been almost completely bought out by the drug companies. The APA could not continue without the pharmaceutical company support of meetings, symposia, workshops, journal advertising, grand rounds luncheons, unrestricted educational grants etc. etc. Psychiatrists have become the minions of drug company promotions.

APA, of course, maintains that its independence and autonomy are not compromised in this enmeshed situation. Anyone with the least bit of common sense attending the annual meeting would observe how the drug company exhibits and industry-sponsored symposia draw crowds with their various enticements while the serious scientific sessions are barely attended.

Psychiatric training reflects their influence as well; i.e., the most important part of a resident's curriculum is the art and quasi-science of dealing drugs, i.e., prescription writing.

These psychopharmacological limitations on our abilities to be complete physicians also limit our intellectual horizons. No longer do we seek to understand whole persons in their social contexts, rather we are there to realign our patients' neurotransmitters. The problem is that it is very difficult to have a relationship with a neurotransmitter, whatever its configuration.

So, our guild organization provides a rationale, by its neuro-biological tunnel vision, for keeping our distance from the molecule conglomerates we have come to define as patients.

We condone and promote the widespread overuse and misuse of toxic chemicals that we know have serious long-term effects: tardive dyskinesia, tardive dementia and serious withdrawal syndromes.

So, do I want to be a drug company patsy who treats molecules with their formulary? No, thank you very much.

It saddens me that after 35 years as a psychiatrist I look forward to being dissociated from such an organization. In no way does it represent my interests.

It is not within my capacities to buy into the current biomedical-reductionistic model heralded by the psychiatric leadership as once again marrying us to somatic medicine. This is a matter of fashion, politics and, like the pharmaceutical house connection, money.

In addition, APA has entered into an unholy alliance with NAMI (I don't remember the members being asked if they supported such an organization) such that the two organizations have adopted similar public belief systems about the nature of madness. While professing itself the champion of their clients the APA is supporting non-clients, the parents, in their wishes to be in control, via legally enforced dependency, of their mad/bad offspring. NAMI, with tacit APA approval, has set out a pro-neuroleptic drug and easy commitment-institutionalization agenda that violates the civil rights of their offspring.

For the most part we stand by and allow this fascistic agenda to move forward. Their psychiatric god, Dr. E. Fuller Torrey, is allowed to diagnose and recommend treatment to those in the NAMI organization with whom he disagrees. Clearly, a violation of medical ethics.

Does APA protest?

Of course not, because he is speaking what APA agrees with but can't explicitly espouse. He is allowed to be a foil; after all he is no longer a member of APA. (Slick work APA!)

The short-sightedness of this marriage of convenience between APA, NAMI and the drug companies (who gleefully support both groups because of their shared pro-drug stance) is an abomination. I want no part of a psychiatry of oppression and social control.

Biologically based brain diseases are convenient for families and practitioners alike.

It is no-fault insurance against personal responsibility. We are just helplessly caught up in a swirl of brain pathology for which no one, except DNA, is responsible. Now, to begin with, anything that has an anatomically defined specific brain pathology becomes the province of neurology (syphilis is an excellent example).

So, to be consistent with this brain disease view all the major psychiatric disorders would become the territory of our neurologic colleagues. Without having surveyed them I believe they would eschew responsibility for these problematic individuals. However, consistency would demand our giving over biologic brain diseases to them. The fact that there is no evidence confirming the brain disease attribution is, at this point, irrelevant.

What we are dealing with here is fashion, politics and money. This level of intellectual/scientific dishonesty is just too egregious for me to continue to support by my membership.

I view with no surprise that psychiatric training is being systemically disavowed by American medical school graduates. This must give us cause for concern about the state of today's psychiatry. It must mean at least in part that they view psychiatry as being very limited and unchallenging. To me it seems clear that we are headed toward a situation in which, except for academics, most psychiatric practitioners will have no real relationships — so vital to the healing process — with the disturbed and disturbing persons they treat.

Their sole role will be that of prescription writers: ciphers in the guise of being "helpers."

Finally, why must the APA pretend to know more than it does?

DSM-IV is the fabrication upon which psychiatry seeks acceptance by medicine in general. Insiders know it is more a political than scientific document. To its credit it says so — although its brief apologia is rarely noted. DSM-IV has become a bible and a money-making best seller, its major failings notwithstanding. It confines and defines practice, some take it seriously, others more realistically.

It is the way to get paid.

Diagnostic reliability is easy to attain for research projects.

The issue is what do the categories tell us? Do they in fact accurately represent the person with a problem? They don't, and can't, because there are no external validating criteria for psychiatric diagnoses.

There is neither a blood test nor specific anatomic lesions for any major psychiatric disorder. So, where are we? APA as an organization has implicitly (sometimes explicitly as well) bought into a theoretical hoax. Is psychiatry a hoax — as practiced today? Unfortunately, the answer is mostly yes.

What do I recommend to the organization upon leaving after experiencing three decades of its history?

To begin with:

1. let us be ourselves. Stop taking on unholy alliances without the members' permission.
2. get real about science, politics and money. Label each for what it is — that is, be honest.
3. get out of bed with NAMI and the drug companies. APA should align itself, if one believes its rhetoric, with the true consumer groups, i.e., the ex-patients, psychiatric survivors etc.
4. talk to the membership. I can't be alone in my views.

We seem to have forgotten a basic principle: the need to be patient/client/consumer satisfaction oriented. I always remember Manfred Bleuler's wisdom: "Loren, you must never forget that you are your patient's employee."

In the end they will determine whether or not psychiatry survives in the service marketplace.

Sincerely,

Loren R. Mosher MD

Appendix II

Accreditations of the Previous Work

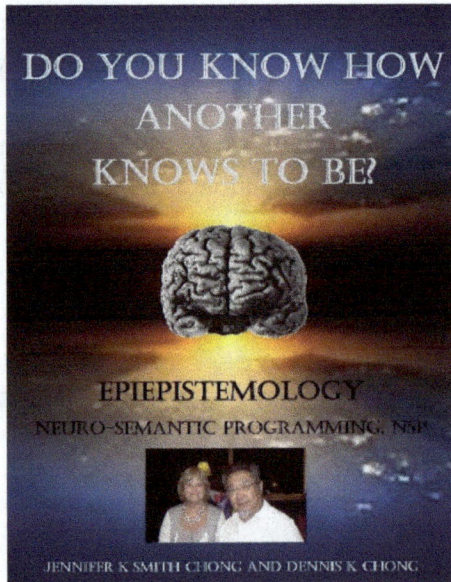

"This book enfolds several critical-scientific approaches to understand the mind-body environment nexus that characterises the human condition. With great eloquence and based on extensive research and knowledge of various disciplines, it presents us with a philosophy and investigative tool: Neuro-Semantic Programming.

It breaks radically from the Aristotelian hierarchical view of the human mind, bringing out its associative and connective structure. Unlike its counterpart, Neuro-Linguistic Programming, NLP, it offers a truly humanistic and human approach to understanding everything from language to pain. This book is a 'must read' by anyone who is interested in what we are."

—Marcel Danesi, PhD, FRS(C)

Professor of Anthropology, University of Toronto

"This tome is a very valuable contribution to the current literature in this area. It clearly illustrates the path of thinking and research that the two authors have brilliantly carried out to publish this work. I find their area of expertise fascinating, thought provoking and very original. They have laid the path of other workers to carry on to develop this field even more for the benefit of mankind; their painstaking effort should be congratulated and applauded."

—Saroja Krishnaswamy, MB, BS, FRANZCP, FRCPsych (UK)

Professor of Psychiatry, University of Western Sydney,

Australia

"This book is simply exquisite. As the authors conclude, its contents may have bodhisattvatistic consequences for the reader."

—George C. Woo, OD, PhD. FAAO, FACO, FCOptom

Former Dean, Faculty of Health and Social Science, Hong Kong Polytechnic University

Emeritus Professor, School of Optometry and Visual Science, University of Waterloo, Ontario

"A wise book, enlightening and powerful."

—Margaret Marsan

"Jennifer and Dennis Chong have exceeded expectation in the collaboration of this book. It is a true masterpiece filled with scientific data and timely information that every healthcare provider should know. Full of useful information. I highly recommend it for every professional library."

—Robert Otto
CEO, International Medical and Dental Hypnotherapy Association

"It provided me (a seasoned clinician) with valuable insights and new perspectives on the following:

- Thinking and language and their importance in communication patterns between human beings
- The structural methods of thinking and thoughts in the mind
- The relevance of insights derived from Quantum Physics and their application in mental functioning
- A good critique of the Aristotelian system of Cause and Effect
- A correct highlight of the Non-Aristotelian Principles of Relativity and Relatedness, emphasizing the importance of the Non-Aristotelian Frame and its utility in psychotherapy."

—Karl O'Sullivan, MD, DPM, FRCP(I), FRCP(C),
FRCPsych(UK). DABPN

"The authors embrace so much information from wide corners of studies and situations. This book brings forth the human aspects which encompass the knowledge necessary for the readers to appreciate where we are (and can be, if pursued further).

Difficult as the subject is, the book gets to the bottom and sides of humanity and thus brings value to all.

This is a specific treatment for our not-so-perfect understanding of what seems to be churning in the world."

—Dato Syed Ahmad Idid
Former Judge of the High Courts of Malaysia

"After I finished reading this book, I felt centered and I then realised that there is more here than one might know or see. There is more there that the world needs to know."

—Steve Corbeil
President, Prime Marine Canada

"This work is staggering in its scope and import."

—Gary Philips, MA, CRSP, CHRP
NLP Trainer

"This work advances the understanding of the human condition and offers the reader a new approach, a Non-Aristotelian approach in being and relating. What is so eloquently put forth is an alternative to current mainstream thinking and communication. The Chongs, however, go beyond the excellence in communication, introducing a new philosophy and a new manner in relating and understanding each other by communicating clearly with honesty and respect."

—Bryan Walsh, MA

Appendix III

The Quantum Vacuum

We came to know about the concept of Quantum Vacuum via the work *Punk Science* by Dr. Manjir Samanta-Laughton.

However, we were already familiar with Heinz Pagels's perspective of what it was that was *before* the beginning of time:

> The nothingness "before" the creation of the universe is the most complete void that we can imagine — no space, time or matter existed. It is a world without place, without duration or eternity, without number — it is what the mathematicians call "the empty set." Yet this unthinkable void converts itself into the plenum of existence — a necessary consequence of physical laws. Where are these laws written into that void? What "tells" the void that it is pregnant with a possible universe? It would seem that even the void is subjected to law, a logic that exists prior to space and time. (Heinz R. Pagels, *Perfect Symmetry: The Search for the Beginning of Time* [New York: Simon & Schuster, 1985], 347)

In past books and articles, we described this "empty set" of Pagels's as the Infinite Void of Empty Nothingness (IVOEN). This was the ultimate vacuum. The concept of Quantum Vacuum postulates that in the Quantum Vacuum there might be no sub-atomic particles of quantum mechanics (QM), but yet it could have an ocean of them. In the Infinite Void of Empty Nothingness, before time, there is *absolutely nothing — not even* QM particles.

From what we know, no physicist has ever said that, after the Big Bang and the unfolding of the universe, our universe *and all other possible universes are suspended* in the Absolute Infinite Vacuum (our term) of the IVOEN. If, as they say, our universe is expanding at near the speed of light, then it is obvious that it is doing so into the Absolute Infinite Vacuum of the IVOEN. It is the Absolute Infinite Vacuum of the IVOEN that is expanding.

We are the products of the laws of physics that determined our universe's evolution; and, logically, these same laws of physics or, more specifically, a subset of them, also determined our unfolding and the evolution of our Being and our lives.

From *Punk Science* can be derived this postulate that all possible knowledge, information, data, things, and other beings are in the Absolute Infinite Vacuum of the IVOEN. As we are limited in our nature, it then follows that our HOPs and An^{Y}14 are the limiting devices that allow what can filter into our brains and our Being and, in doing so, unfold our reality to us. This is how it is in accord with the sight of Humberto Maturana and Francisco Varela, that each of us has *a* world but not *the* world.

Appendix IV

C→E

Below are the eminences who have repudiated Cause and Effect (C→E). In the latter half of the twentieth century, the case for the discontinuation of C→E was established. Doubts about C→E were advanced as far back as 1777 by David Hume, who wrote:

> But when one particular species of event has always, in all instances, been conjoined with another, we make no longer any scruple of foretelling one upon the appearance of the other, and of employing that reasoning, which can alone assure us of any matter of fact or existence. We then call the one object *Cause*; the other, *Effect*. We suppose that there is some connexion [sic] between them; some power in the one, by which it infallibly produces the other, and operates with the greatest certainty and strongest necessity.
>
> It appears, then, that this idea of a necessary connexion among events arises from a number of similar instances which occur of the constant conjunction of these events; nor can that idea ever be suggested by any one of these instances, surveyed in all possible lights and positions. But there is nothing in a number of instances, different from every single instance, which is supposed to be exactly similar; except only, that after a repetition of similar instances, the mind is carried

by habit, upon the appearance of one event, to expect its usual attendant, and to believe that it will exist. This connexion, therefore, which we *feel* in the mind, this customary transition of the imagination from one object to its usual attendant, is the sentiment or impression from which we form the idea of power or necessary connexion. Nothing farther is in the case. (David Hume, *Concerning Human Understanding and Concerning the Principles of Morals* [Oxford: Clarendon Press, 1979], 74–75).

Then, in 1933, Alfred Korzybski questioned the validity of C→E:

We "feel," and try to "think," about "cause and effect" as *contiguous* in "time." But "contiguous in time" involves the impossible "infinitesimal" of some unit of "time." But, since we have seen that there is no such thing, we must accept that the interval between "cause" and "effect" is finite. This structural fact changes the whole situation. If the interval between "cause" and "effect" is finite, then always something might happen between, no matter how small the interval may be. The "same cause" would not produce the "same effect." The expected result would not follow. (Alfred Korzybski, *Science and Sanity* [The International Non-Aristotelian Library Publishing Company, 1958], 216).

Then in 1975, the fathers of Neuro-Linguistic Programming wrote the most castigating take of the language of C→E, as follows:

We have generalised the notion of semantic ill-formedness to include sentences such as

My husband makes me mad.

The therapist can identify this sentence as having the form

Some person causes some person to have some emotion.

When the first person, the one doing the causing, is different from the person experiencing the anger, the sentence is said to be semantically ill-formed and unacceptable. The semantic ill-formedness ... arises because it, literally, is not possible for one human being to create an emotion in another human being ... The act itself does not cause the emotion; ... the emotion is a response generated from a model in which the client takes no responsibility for experiences which he *could* control. (Richard Bandler and John Grinder, *The Structure of Magic* [Science and Behaviour Books Inc., 1975], 51–52).

Then in 1980 Arthur Koestler put forward this critique of C→E:

Absolute space and absolute time had already gone overboard; and the third pillar of our traditional view of the world, the law of causal determination, now follow suit. The so-called Laws of Nature lost their solid character; they could no longer be regarded as expressing certainties, merely statistical probabilities. The rigid causal connections between "cause" and "effect" were loosened, softened up as it were; what the physicist had regarded as universal laws now turned out to be mere rules of the thumb, whose validity was limited to medium-sized phenomena; on the sub-atomic level ... all certainty vanished from the universe. (Arthur Koestler, *Bricks to Babel: Selected Writings with comments by the author* [London: Hutchinson & Co. (Publishers) Ltd., 1980], 77–78).

Then, in our book, *Don't Ask WHY?!*, we offered this insight:

Cause/effect thinking creates inconsistencies. It creates misperceptions that become incorporated into the definition of ourselves as individuals and as society. For by thinking in cause/effect, we perceive in cause/effect and vice versa. Previous attempts to remove cause/effect from language failed as a new language system was necessary. (Dennis K. Chong & Jennifer K. Chong, *Don't Ask WHY?!: A Book About the Structure of Blame, Bad Communication and Miscommunication* [Ontario: C-Jade Publications Inc., 1991], 7).

This was followed by the critique of C→E by the physicist David C. Cassidy, who wrote this about the "causality principle":

The causality principle requires that every effect be preceded by a unique cause. This idea had served for over a century as a basic assumption of practically every form of rational research. ...

The uncertainty principle, Heisenberg asserted, denies this: "in the strict formulation of the causal law — if we know the present, we can calculate the future — it is not the conclusion that is wrong but the premise. ... he causal connection between the present and the future is lost, and the laws and predictions of quantum mechanics become probabilistic...

Heisenberg's uncertainty principle was profound and far-reaching in nearly every respect. (David C. Cassidy, *Heisenberg, Uncertainty and the Quantum Revolution* [Scientific American, May 1992], 110–111).

Appendix V

Asking Questions

In all of us is our default assumption that we know what question to ask. Everyone wants to ask the right question. If our question is right, then we will get the right answer. With the right answer we will be on track to do the right thing. In this way, we ensure that we will not be blamed for doing the wrong thing.

From our second reading of the *Symposium* in Plato's *Six Great Dialogues*, we have come to learn from Socrates that it is far more important to be able to ask good questions than it is to ask right questions; the ultimate achievement is to be able to ask the good question! What is the good question? It is the question that will peel open for you the true nature of a problem.

Unless it was by good chance, none of us has ever asked a question that peeled open the nature of a problem. However, Socrates, in the *Symposium*, showed how the logical sequence of his good questions, invariably, took him to the good question. With it, with the true nature of the problem before him, he could then proceed to solve the contentious problem that was at the very heart of the debate between two elites of ancient Athenian society.

When reading the *Symposium* the second time, we had with us the mastery of the language of the Aristotelian System of Cause and Effect, the language of the Non-Aristotelian System of Relativity and Relatedness, the Modified Meta Model, the language formats of

Informal Logic, the language of Body Language, Non-Verbal Communication, Calibration, Adumbration, and the skill to read the Core Persona of another (i.e., the person-to-context). With this, we had the Virtual Philosophies of all these language systems and, by extension, the logic of these language systems. In this way, as we read the *Symposium*, we knew immediately the structure by which Socrates formulated his questions.

In the six months before we retired (on December 18, 2018), I (Dennis) had fifty new patients. Therefore, I set off to see if I could solve the problems of my patients just by asking Socratic questions. I was so very pleased that I was able to do so. We decided to write a book on asking questions, *Just Like Socrates*.

People ask questions on the fly; in other words, they use their own idea of what they think the semantics of a context are, in which a problem is being exacerbated. Of course, this is an opinion. Next, they use their common sense, native linguistic skill, and native semantic intuitions to determine what question to ask.

For a start, one cannot rely on common sense. What is the proof? The proof is that, for centuries, common sense told us that the sun rose from the east and set in the west. Common sense also confirmed to us that the earth is flat. After all, we stood on it and did not fall over. When the sun sank below the horizon, we prayed that it would travel successfully through the underworld and rise again in the East. When it was realised that the earth was not flat, common sense then told us that the sun revolved around the earth. Common sense told us that we were at the centre of the universe. It also told us that we are the only living sentient creatures in our universe; and so continued the other nonsenses that common sense told us.

If we rely on common sense, we will never be able to ask good questions let alone *the good question*.

To be able to ask good questions and, especially, the good question, a person has to have a broad and deep philosophy of life. The answer is found in the languages they use. Each language has its Virtual Philosophy (VP). Currently, you have only the Virtual

Philosophy of the Aristotelian System of Cause and Effect (A) and the Virtual Philosophy of Informal Logic (IL). It is by your versions of A and IL that their power has propelled you into your unique trajectory of life and, finally, to the orbit of your life.

If you were to acquire the Virtual Philosophies of the Non-Aristotelian System of Relativity and Relatedness (Ã), the metalanguage of the Modified Meta Model (3M) and the No-Y-ian Model of Language (~YML), you would be amazed at the benefits of various physical, emotional, and mental layers. Additionally, you will need the Virtual Philosophies of being able to read Body Language, Non-Verbal Communication, Adumbration, Calibration, and the specific Core Reading of a person's personhood.

When you master these languages, their VPs will automatically become a part of you. Your thinking will change and, with it, you will be on the road to ask contrarian questions and then good questions and, eventually, you find your ability to ask the Good Question.

Appendix VI

Virtual Philosophy

What is a Virtual Philosophy? Western culture is a paradigm. We (as authors) were brought up in it. We live it. If you were brought up in it too, you may think you know the philosophy of Western culture well. But do you? Likely not. If you're like most people, you probably know how to give fine and astute opinions about it. However, an opinion about X is *not* X.

When we live in a *system*, we are a part of it. By its Virtual Philosophy, we automatically and unconsciously live by it and its language. Its language carries its logic, syntax/rules, and grammar. By the act of using its language, we are *one* with it.

En passant language is a problem amidst a host of biddy, little life problems. Thus, it is a problem both for immigrants and for the Indigenous people of the host country. It is especially so if the alien language is far older than that of the Indigenous population, for example, by thousands of years. The immigrants will resist learning the language of the host country. I (Dennis) know this for a fact because part of my family were immigrants from China to the British Protectorate of Malaya (currently Malaysia). One part of my family would not learn English or Malay. The part that did were deemed to have betrayed their ancestors. So, they were shunned by the part that did not. It was years later, when I was in my early fifties, that I found that I had Chinese-speaking family in Malaysia that I knew nothing about. I have since amended this.

If there is any semantic glitch, flaw, or negativity intrinsic in the system of language, its negative consequences will unfurl around the lives of everyone in a given community, and all will live it. Thus, from our current language, out of E^{epi}/NSP, we now know of our insanity to have expectations. Amazingly, we have expectations in a reality in which everything is *unknown* — and in spite of the fact that there are no guarantees, certainties, or sureties. Think! In such a reality, how on Earth can you have *expectations*, let alone *entitlements*?

The odd thing is that, regardless of the negativities and downsides of the system that we are in, we will automatically *adapt to them, adjust to them, habituate to them, get used to them*, and finally, *accommodate them*. When we accommodate them, then we will have the full repertoire of Language Structures to explain, rationalise, reason, justify, and amplify how it is that all the negative consequences are perfectly natural, normal, regular, as it should be, and just as God would will it!

What is the proof of this? One thing few people know is that human warfare is a part of the Aristotelian System of Cause and Effect. From Day One, we have always used its language, and we now come to realise that from A evolves a critical phenomenon. What is this critical phenomenon? It is *blame*.

By way of *blame*, we can give a look that kills, words that kill — metaphorically — and actions that *physically kill*. Of course, you can kill because of your anger, rage, or fury. However, you can kill only one person at a time given that the emotions of anger, rage, and fury in and of themselves will consume vast amounts of energy Of course, in the time of mass shootings and bombings, the gun or bomb replaces the energy required for the physical act and, thus, many now can be killed en masse.

However, when you kill by blame, you will have lots of spare energy to do lots of killing. The records validate that, the night before the Battle of Waterloo, there was a grand dinner for Marshal Arthur Wellesley and the entire officer corps of the British Army. This was followed by a grand ball. Next morning, the officers were with their regiments and companies — and then they were off to do their killing.

We have always been steeped in the activity of human warfare. Did you know, in the slaughter of the battles of the Crusades, the clarion call for the Christian side was always *As God wills it!* This granted Crusaders the legitimacy to slaughter. Is it a comfort to know that God wants you to kill?

On Wednesday, December 11, 2019, we happened to see the Headline News program of the RT TV channel. In this program, the newscaster scathingly attacked Presidents Bush, Obama, and Trump for their rationalizations, reasons, and amplifications for the twenty-year US war in Afghanistan. To the newscaster, what was blatantly obvious was that the military of the US had failed to win the war. All the verbal iterations by these three US presidents were *lies* told to the American public.

It has cost US citizens trillions and a significant amount of treasure. Who profited? The Pentagon, the political elite, and the US Military Industrial Complex.

The Authors

Jennifer & Dennis Chong
Fellows of the Society of Neuro-Semantics
Fellows of the American Board of Psychotherapy
Fellows of the Medical and Dental Hypnosis Association

We shared a conjoint practice in Therapy and Hypnosis from 1979 to 2018. By our exploration, examination, and inquiry into the fields of Ontology, Epistemology, Linguistics, Philosophy, Semantics, Syntax, Grammar, Chaos Theory, Systems Theory, Game Theory, Cybernetics, Religion, Morality and Ethics, and Science and Cosmology, we discovered the new field of Epiepistemology. It is so named, in the tradition of the Greek word, in honour of the ancient Greek philosophers who first signposted for us the direction of our research.

Other Works

The authors have published or are soon to publish books in the following categories:

Philosophy

Don't Ask WHY?!: A Book About the Structure of Blame, Bad Communication and Miscommunication

A glimpse at forever a chance for eternity: I, the ultimate nominalization, or TO BE

There Is No God — an NSP Response (forthcoming)

Linguistics

Power and Elegance in Communication

Just Like Socrates (forthcoming)

Hypnosis and the Language of Hypnosis

The Knife Without Pain

Sociology

Well-Being Health and Happiness

Neuro-Semantic Programming

Do You Know How Another Knows to Be?

Therapeutic Algorithms

Human Nature — Is It Possible to Change It?

Acknowledgements

We would like to acknowledge the following wonderful souls for their contribution to the making of our book:

First, to our close friends Bazyli and Yusra Debowski for their assistance in initiating the prospect and project of the writing process.

Next, to Hashan Shen for the front cover of our book.

To Lee Parpart and Colborne Communications for their stellar work in editing the rough drafts to the final edit.

To Cheryl Hawley and Paula Chiarcos who did the layout and proofreading after final edits were made.

Finally, to our friend Rob Blom for his countless hours, days, and months of service in helping us edit and format the book to its final completion.

Index